Dear Thomas,
With thanks for your friendship and generous spirit.
I hope you'll enjoy this book every day of the year — for years to come.

With big hugs,

Psalmistry

Reflections of Praise

E.J. Emerson

WestBow Press
A DIVISION OF THOMAS NELSON
& ZONDERVAN

Copyright © 2017 E.J. Emerson.

All rights reserved. No part of this book may be used or reproduced by any means, graphic, electronic, or mechanical, including photocopying, recording, taping or by any information storage retrieval system without the written permission of the publisher except in the case of brief quotations embodied in critical articles and reviews.

WestBow Press books may be ordered through booksellers or by contacting:

WestBow Press
A Division of Thomas Nelson & Zondervan
1663 Liberty Drive
Bloomington, IN 47403
www.westbowpress.com
1 (866) 928-1240

Because of the dynamic nature of the Internet, any web addresses or links contained in this book may have changed since publication and may no longer be valid. The views expressed in this work are solely those of the author and do not necessarily reflect the views of the publisher, and the publisher hereby disclaims any responsibility for them.

Any people depicted in stock imagery provided by Thinkstock are models, and such images are being used for illustrative purposes only. Certain stock imagery © Thinkstock.

ISBN: 978-1-4908-1335-6 (sc)
ISBN: 978-1-4908-1336-3 (hc)
ISBN: 978-1-4908-1334-9 (e)

Library of Congress Control Number: 2013919027

Printed in the United States of America.

WestBow Press rev. date: 11/21/2017

To my late friend and favorite nag,
Leo Carolan

And to my beloved friend
who now sings in heaven's choirs,
Amanda Newhouse Carnie

PREFACE

Admiration, commendation, tribute, acclaim, applause, devotion: these are just a few synonyms for *praise*. Praise is focused on the object of appreciation, and so we expect psalms of praise to always be focused on God. But praise comes as expressions of gratitude more closely tied to the speaker's point of view.

We who are people of faith, living in a dynamic, intimate relationship with the Creator of the universe, have the opportunity to bend God's ear at any time. This conversation, which is never only one-way, is the privilege we call prayer. Sometimes praise looks more like lament, or complaint, or an emotional tantrum, yet praise it remains, for without the special awe we hold for God, we would never even think to bring such plaintive woes to our prayer conversation with the Lord.

One Sunday morning in January, as a student pastor delivering my first public sermon, I challenged the congregation to give up the foolish tradition of making New Year's resolutions, vows we are sure to break. Let's begin each day instead by singing a new song to God, I said. It was an earnest message that was warmly received. Three weeks later, as I was driving to my office job, the Holy Spirit burst into my preoccupied mind: "Where is my new song?" Nonplussed and a bit disoriented, but never at a loss for words, I responded, "Huh?" The patient Spirit said, more plainly still, "Where is my new song? You promised me a *new song* every day." I began this book that day.

These personal psalms are a labor of love and devotion, a record of gratitude, *kvetch* and worship. They are a testimony to the awesome love and tenderness with which our Lord teaches us, opens our eyes, and informs our hearts. I hope this collection will serve to guide many in daily devotion. My prayer is that it will also challenge more than a few readers to begin writing your own new songs to our incomparable God.

In addition to thanking God our Parent, Jesus our Christ, and the only muse I know, God's Spirit, I owe a huge debt of gratitude to many mentors, encouragers, test readers and editors.

- First and foremost, my mother and best friend Sandy Emerson, who lovingly watched me along my journey of faith, and has never failed to encourage, educate or upbraid, as needed;
- My mentors, creatively gifted pastors, teachers and friends: Tom Bartha, Dianne Clark, John and Margaret Coakley, Jill Fenske, Paul Fries, Renee House, Jim Knol, Mark Kraai, H. Joon Lee, Carol Mutch, Andy Rienstra, Beverly Sulliphant, and Virginia Wiles;
- I fear I would not have had the stamina to see the project through to completion without the unflagging support and honest critiques of dear friends Peggy Campbell, Penilyn Kruge, Dale Kent, the late Kip Lester, Bart Spears, Elizabeth Vaneekhoven, and fellow poets Maude Carolan Pych and Betty Marchitti;
- I am grateful to all at WestBow Press who have helped me bring this book into print;
- Finally, it seems fitting to end with a nod to my favorite curmudgeon Leo Carolan for provoking me from time to time with honest criticism spoken in love while he was still among us.

UNCONNECTED

What a way to start a year!
Lord, I am fed up
With people's disregard,
Especially in public places
Designated for quiet.
You know what I mean!
The cell phones, the candy wrappers,
The loud voices, shouts, boisterous noise,
The coming and going, like tides,
The running commentaries in inside places
Using outside voices—I want to scream,
"This is NOT your LIVING ROOM!"

But then, Lord,
You make me see
I'm wrong.
Because home is not where family lives,
No longer a place for group hugs,
Conversation, discussion, and whoops
Of joy or shrieks of delight.
Living rooms? No more.
Everyone is isolated
With personal electronics.
So when kids flock to the movies,
As the film runs, they feel free
To jump rows, run the aisle,
Open and close doors, even bolt outside
As though their performance
Were part of the entertainment

We all paid to see.
It doesn't matter, I see now,
This lack of continuity in their screening,
The interruptions, the noise, the tumult—
They are victims of ADD, just
As schools and doctors would say;
Yet not as they mean it,
For the disease that holds them in sway
Is their parents' Attention Deficit for them.
There is no more living
Room
At home
No breathing
Room
No sharing;
Only supplies, resources
And half-hearted rules
Seldom enforced.
Families are unconnected,
Deconstructed,
So kids intrude
On strangers
To display their pain.
Negative attention
Is better than none,
I hear.

Show me new ways,
My Lord,
To love these noisy broken souls.

VOICES

The human voice is such a miracle
Soft as baby cheeks,
Mountain mist rising from dawn-lit lakes,
Moss on old stone walls;
Strong as bellowing bulls,
Thunderclaps, stampeding herds,
Niagara Falls;
From rumble to roar
From hover to soar
You have given us a glimpse of heaven
In our own instrument of praise.

January 3

POWDER & STEEL

The heavens are sagging this morning
Drooping, dragging, scraping bottom
Like a cozy old overstuffed sofa,
Lining split and guts hanging down
Layer upon layer of batting
Thick ropes, some twisted for strength,
Some burst and frayed by wear
Splaying splintered fingers
Spilling comfort across the floor.
A low ceiling, they say, this cloud cover,
This endless and infinitely mutable duvet
Quilted with wisps of thistle,
Bisque, lavender, and smoke,
Orchid, and ivory, pewter, slate,
Seashell, powder and steel.

Most look up to see only rain
Poised in pregnant thunderheads
About to burst open upon them
A drenching iron curtain.

Some sense instead a sea of cotton
A gentle panorama, an invitation to explore.
Tuck me in, Lord, and rock me gently:
I want to close my eyes and nestle
Into this featherbed You have laid out
Over me, this warm fleece of love.

PENSIVE

A pot of pansies.
Thoughtful faces:
Intense, inquisitive,
Perky, poking heads;
Slender, craning necks;
Purple eyelashes
Yellow cheeks
Half-open mouths
Poised to speak
The secrets of spring.

PATIENCE

Some folks wait well
Quiet, docile, meek,
Patient enough to seek
Distraction, they tell
Of a pleasant time
Observing life on pause.
Some folks explode in line,
Pushing and shoving, because
Crowds fence and hedge,
Hobble their progress
And double their stress,
Driving them to the edge.
Patience is more than merit
It is serenity, and peace of mind,
A calm spirit able to inherit
Tolerance and mercy in place of pride.

VERACITY

It takes perspicacity
To detect mendacity,
But there's a paucity
Of folks with sagacity.
Accuse me of audacity,
But spare me opacity:
For I treasure veracity.
Whether it's voracity
Or even, gulp, rapacity,
I admit my capacity
For Truth grows as it's fed,
Filling both heart and head.

WORDS

The preacher stacks them
As inviting steps toward the Light.
The writer pushes them
Across the page, winging flight.
The politician tweaks them
And beats them, then cheats them
Into pretense and false devotion.
The teacher marches them
And drills them like timbrels:
Pretty, practical, clever and fun.
The journalist explodes them
In 70-point type to catch the eye
And pause the breath of all who read.
The executive metes them out,
Speech and memo, in quotable form.
The composer orchestrates them
In harmony or counterpoint,
Always with perfect pitch.
The poet strings them,
Lustrous pearls. Compelling,
Beguiling, round and warm,
Beautiful enough to hide their flaws.
The Bible lifts them, drops them,
Unfolds them in story, in prayer,
In psalm, in teaching, in warning
And lament. Here they are all one
Word, Your Word, Yourself revealed.
Oh, give us eyes to see!

KEEPING SILENCE

My body is silent,
My mouth in repose.
My eyes are closed,
But my brain is wide open
And just won't shut up!
Words, images, connections
Buzz around like dust
Suspended in a shaft of light.
Quiet my mind,
Reverence my soul,
Keep me silent before You, Lord,
My God,
That I may hear
Your every word.

GRASS

In a cool blue pool of shadow
Stands a brilliant expanse of green
Where morning sun pours down
On the sequin-studded lawn
Shimmering and sparkling
As a breeze strolls through.
Some blades stand tall,
Fully erect, smugly stretched
Skyward, while the many others
Bend, bowing their heads.
It is they who bear drops of dew
Glistening on their backs.
I know science will explain
That once the dew rolls down
By gravity to the soil,
The grass can rise up straight.
But today I see so clearly, Lord,
It is the humble, grateful ones—
Those showing reverence before You,
Throwing open their arms in praise—
Who receive Your sustaining grace;
While those who despise Your gifts
In their self-righteous head-high pride
Will be the first to fall before the scythe.

January 10

LEGS

Stools have three for balance;
Chairs and tables, usually four.
For fight or flight, most creatures
Have them, whether two, four, six
Or many, for one is seldom enough—
Though the case can be made
That one is sufficient to stand on.
A smash hit on Broadway has *legs*,
Though perhaps not dancer gams.
Even wine has *legs* in a glass
When it swirls, coats and clings.

When we realize we need help
To achieve our desires and dreams,
To move ahead and get a leg up,
We go to others for advice, assistance,
Alliance. But too often we have to be
On our last legs to approach You,
The only One with our true welfare
In mind, the only One able to save us
With a mighty hand. For it is when
We come to You on our knees
That you raise us to stand on our own
Two feet, and lead us to walk,
One humble leg at a time.

EVIDENCE

Alone
Spindly legs akimbo
A tiny heap lies dead center
In the road, white tail tucked
Under his spotted rump.
This is murder,
I'm thinking,
Slowing
to drive around;
Evisceration by motor vehicle.
Where is the police tape?
Why no flashing lights?
No investigation?
To find the brute
Who mowed down
Ploughed over
Ripped open
Shattered the bones
Stopped the breath
Extinguished the light
Of this woodland waif?
Lord, I don't know how to pray
I am so angry,
So offended,
my heart
Ripped open.
Mowed down.
Ploughed over.
Shattered.
Dragged
to that
dark
place
where
Only Your light remains.
And yet there is my hope,
My Lord, Your light remains.

ANGER

Banked and cooled, the fire
Seems dead;
No color lingers among the greys
Of charcoal, ash and charred bark,
Not even a tiny glimmer of red
No wisp of smoke
No faint crackle of consumption
Yet
At the first slap of hot wind
Against the cold fuel
Hidden embers spark
Hungry flames arise
Capable of devouring all in their path.
Dormant anger is defiant
Destructive
Devastating
Dying only when no fuel is left
No air, no breath
No burn.
Lord, put this anger into a vacuum
And stifle it for good.
Rain down grace and mercy
To transform the ever-present embers
Into a rich soil of rebirth.

NIGHT SOUNDS

A sudden change in atmosphere
Brings a slight bout of asthma
Wheezing, whistling like a steam valve
I dig under the quilt to muffle the chill
And warm the rattle in my breast.
One cat purrs, pressed against me,
But her murmur is fright-induced,
Not relaxed,
Rhythmically she produces a whir,
A flutter, not quite a growl,
An unhappy flap-flap rap.
The other cat is genuinely joyful,
Generating a wing-like flutter,
An undercurrent, an accompaniment.
Outside, the source of one companion's
Terror: shingle-shaking, ground-grumbling
Rippling, rumbling roars overhead,
And the rain drumming, pounding, thrumming,
Hammering down. What fine bedfellows
We make, we noisemakers, sounding off
Quite naturally, unintentionally,
Harmonically in point/counterpoint
With an occasional syncopated beat.
But we are not improvising an invention;
The notes, the cadence, the pulse,
The breath
Are all from You.
Maestro,
All from You.

SHOWER OF LIGHT

In the penumbra of early
    morning
Après shower, bath dimmed
By a failed light
Illuminated only by flashlight,
A limited reach,
My myopic eyes detect
    movement.
A crawl overhead,
A swirl of shadow and glow
Toward the narrow edge
Of the closed door:
The slender boundary of dark
From bright.
Rather than reach for foggy
    lenses,
I squint, cringing slightly,
At the creepy silhouette
Swarming across the ceiling
And spilling over the ill-fit door.
I am haunted yet intrigued
As I peer up at this murky dance,
Suddenly realizing this is steam
Sneaking its way out,
Dissipating into the hall,
Disseminating its moist
    molecules
Throughout the house.
This smoke,
That sets off the detector as it
    passes,
Is merely vapor,
A momentary haze
That mists the mirror
Until cooler air prevails.
So much like our problems, Lord,
Our terrors, frights, worries,
    concerns:
They corner our attention,
They set off our alarms,
They rush our hormones,
Clouding judgment
As we shiver in the dark...

Yet all the while You stand
    waiting,
Just across the sill,
Arms outstretched to take our
    burdens,
Light, Your light,
Beckoning us to step out in faith
And leave the gloom behind.

BREAD OF REMEMBRANCE

In the silence
The yeasty, flavorful rye
Is more fragrant
With every bite.
It has body, this bread;
Each chewy caraway seed
Yields a new burst of taste;
A memory of childhood gathering
At the family table.
Deli lunches, mustard and pickles.
Dry crusts for the duck pond.
Communion
With You
With life
With heritage
With the future
And the glorious possibility
Of the now.
Come, Lord Jesus!
Your body,
My body,
Feed me.

January 16

USELESS

Wheatlike weedy grass
Pokes through the cement
And between the bricks
At the church parking lot.
The early sun is already bright
In the late summer Sunday sky.
Plump sparrows, bold in number,
Delight in their breakfast
Craning to reach
Or hopping up
To pull the tall blades down
Until every edible bit is plucked
Then the bunch moves on
To a clump of fuzzy blond caterpillars
Atop strawlike strands, as animated
As the ceaseless sparrows.
For a moment, as I watch,
In a puddle of sun spilled out
Upon the sidewalk,
The birds stop gleaning to preen.
They chirp, cheep, twitter and tweet...
While I swell with joy.
Thank you, Almighty Lord,
For showing me so clearly today
That nothing in Your creation,
Not even the scruffiest weed,
The forgotten untended grass,
The unkempt beard of the world,
Absolutely nothing is useless
For You created with purpose.

ABOUT HANDS

Reflecting on the work of Frederick Franck at Pacem in Terris (Warwick, NY)

Hands welcome
Hands bar the way
Hands caress
Hands slap around
Hands help
Hands impede
Hands express
Hands halt
Hands hold
Hands reject
Hands uplift
Hands strike down
Hands reach out
Hands refuse
Hands can do only
As our hearts and minds will
Hands kill
Hands nurture
Hands shred

Hands unite
Hands insult
Hands applaud
Your strong hands, Lord,
Which create, build, teach
    and heal,
Your gentle hands are impaled
By our hatred, prejudice,
    violence,
Narcissism, and bellicose revolt;
Your pierced hands spill
The blood that cleans us
The love that saves us
The grace that makes us whole,

So our hands
Can grasp Your hands;
So our hands
Can be Your hands to our world.

SANCTUARY

Silence is a labyrinth.
As I draw more toward the center
I want to drop crumbs
To be sure I can find the way home.
As I venture closer, Lord,
Be my Light,
Hold my hand,
Guide my steps,
Quiet my fears.
As I bask in Your love,
Let me seek sanctuary in Your arms

PLIANT

Lord, when I am lazy, shame me to the plow
When I am angry, keep me from doing harm
When I am petulant, pinch my pouting lips
And when I am rigid, bend me to be pliant
When I am cocky, take me to my knees
When I am rude, remind me how it feels
When I am selfish, break my heart
When I am rigid, mend me to be pliant
Where fear controls minds, send me to teach
Where there is no praise, send me to sing
Where some are misguided, send me to lead
Where others are rigid, take me in Your hands
And let me always be pliant.

FRIENDSHIP

The belt that holds trousers up;
The stitching that quilts the patches;
The simmered stock that makes great stew;
The seasoned bark that shields the trees;
The wiring that brings current to light;
The snuggle, the pat, the squeeze,
The hug in times of need;
The shuffle of tired feet
And pinch of back or knees;
Company in solitude or grief;
Rejoicing at celebration time;
The right fit even when there are gaps;
Platinum, when the market's crashed;
Fencemaking, fencemending, fencebreaking,
According to need—but no fencesitting
Where friendship is found.
Thank You, Lord, for creating us, as we are,
For covenant, cooperation and community.
Thank You, Lord, for crafting our hands
To clasp one another's with such ease.
Thank You, Lord, for transforming our hearts
So we can thrive together in loving peace.

PRIMA LA MUSICA

Prima la musica e poi le parole
Music first and then the words,
The title of one Italian opera claims.
Can we say which came first?
I wonder. I dream. I listen.
Perhaps the music that hums
And throbs and soars its way
Into our hearts—for surely it swells
Our breast before it reaches our mind—
Perhaps it echoes the chant of cherubim
And seraphim, filtering from heaven
Through thunder and drumming rain,
The rustle of breeze-combed wheat,
The gentle whir of pigeon wings,
The step of whitetails on autumn leaves.
It is seductive to think the music of the spheres
Led us to dance our thoughts into language.
But You remind me, *Maestro de tutti maestri*,
That all of creation, including all music,
Was spoken into being by Your Word.

LET GO

Laid off, downsized, pink slipped, given notice, let go...
They bludgeon us with such gentle language.
But, Lord, You are the Master of our lives,
And it is You who know when the time is right
To push us out of the nest we have cozied into,
In spite of our pathetic cries of "Not now!"
As we plummet, beak first,
If we fail to flap, You will catch us
With a warm thermal eased under our wings
Until we relax and let You lift.
Or maybe You let us plunge
From that lofty perch
So we can learn to look up
Let go
And refocus on the One we serve,
Our only true Employer.

January 23

BRIDGES

Bridges carry us over dangerous crossroads,
Chasms, ravines and torrents;
Bridges span alien, unnegotiable terrain;
They hoist us into heavenly perspectives;
Bridges join the unconnected, and bring the distant near;
Bridges are sometimes direct, other times a sinewy way;
They may suspend us, shaking in the wind;
They may cantilever us, firmly anchored;
Bridges always take us where we are going
Yet allow us the possibility to turn back.

Thank You, Lord, for being my Bridge today.

CHILDREN THAT WE ARE...

We run to You with our bumps and booboos;
You kiss it and make it better.
We bring You broken toys, and broken dreams;
You soothe us, then fix, replace or explain.
We come to You desperate and wailing;
You cradle us in Your arms and rock.
We come to You angry and flailing;
You take our blows until we stop.
We plead for Your attention and praise,
We howl for revenge on bullies and brutes,
We scream about all that isn't fair,
We beg and wheedle, smiling pretty,
We offer deals and cross our hearts—
Then grab what You give, shove off,
And run out to brag on what we got.
The next tumble comes a breath later.
Our thanks, our praise, our love
Are scrooged away like trading cards.

Thank You, Lord, for Your merciful patience.
Open Your arms—we come to love You back.
Open Your eyes to see us return thanks
By loving the kids who beat us up and steal our toys.
Open Your ears for our songs of joyful praise.

MUSIC IN THE AIR

The whisper of curtains on a spring night
The cats' purring snore along my hip
The register's rattle as the heat thrums up
The coxswain call of geese soaring by:
There's music in the air.
Puppy snuffles and squeals in a heap
Kid chatter and laughter spilling up the street
Jackhammers, pavers, sweepers and drills
Crows commenting on the latest news:
Noise is music, too.
Woodwinds, brass, strings, keyboard, drums;
Salsa, tango, rap, rock, blues and folk,
Hip-hop, country, Cajun, baroque,
Lullaby, love song, jingle or hymn,
Johnny One-Note or thousand-voice choir,
In Your creation, Lord, there's always music in the air!

SMALL WORDS

Some days I'm worded out
Embarrassed by the paucity of praise
In my purse
Brain-tired
Creatively challenged...
But my heart heaves its sighs
And Your Spirit catches them in flight
Transforming those grunts into
Exultations
Worthy of You
My Lord and Maker
Poet of the Universe
My Teacher.

WINTER TREES

Some see them as life's wretched scrub,
Standing roadside, pitifully mute and disheveled,
Bony arms outstretched in supplication,
Skeletal fingers so spread to receive that they waste
What rains down on them from heaven.

To others, they are elegant elders,
Shoulders stooped a bit under the strain of years,
Tresses thinned by autumns past,
Arthritis and all, limbs lifted heavenward in silent praise
For the God-sent ermine shielding their slender arms.
They know with patient faith,
They know with inexorable assurance,
They know as the sunlight twines new life into their twigs,
They know, oh Lord, they know...
Each winter month is but a day,
And Easter's exaltation is a mere two days away.

MORNING SNOW

The fat wet flakes this morning, Lord,
Falling silently from the still grey air,
Remind me that each and every one,
One of countless billions since the dawn of time,
Each one is,
Like the stars in the heavens,
Like the grains of sand at the shore,
Each one is, no matter how large the crowd,
Unique.

And we, Your children, are
Like each fleeting flake of heaven-tatted lace,
Unique;
From the whorls of our fingertips
To the rungs of our DNA ladder,
Your design for each of us is a one and only.

Thank You, Lord Almighty, for making me unique…
and uniquely Yours.
Thank You that, unlike these momentary masterpieces
falling about me,
I was made for eternity.

THE LORD'S DAY

We call this Your day
The Christian Sabbath, day of rest, day of worship,
Day of praise, prayer and communion.
First day of our week, not the last;
A day to recommit ourselves to Your service
A day to remember our place in the family of faith
A day to revitalize, refocus, recall our purpose
A day to rededicate our resources to You
A day to return to You a portion of what we have
A day to reflect on how we can better serve You.
A day to recharge our batteries, worn down by the world.
This is the day You have made.
We will rejoice and be glad in it.
This day
Your day
Our day
Sunday
Sun day
Son's day.

SLEEP

It's the time the workmen come
Toolboxes in hand
To repair the day's damage
To caulk the stress cracks and shore up what sags.
It's the time the angels come
To soothe the hurts and bind the wounds.
It's the time the world recedes
And dreams come:
The time our busy-ness ceases
Our protests become whispers
And we hear Your voice most clearly.
Thank You, dear God, for sleep
For restful restoration and night vision.
Thank You for revealing to us
In the nocturnal movies You author
What is wrong with the roles we write for ourselves.

January 31

MAILBOXES

Mail receptacles take many shapes, Lord.
Metal bins, with mouths that gape and—gulp!—
The letter is gone.
Slits in doors, flaps on walls that creak and chime;
Khaki baskets, cardboard crates, cubbyholes;
Modems and carriers that bleep, bing and chirp,
Mercurial chat rooms and Hermetic instant flyers:
Messages go Out...
Messages come In...
But nothing is better than my direct link
To You, my God.
You are the carrier, the data, the flow,
You are the operating system and the message,
You are the paper and the ink.
You are my mailbox and my mail.
Your hand is always near, to open my letter;
Your eye has always read before I write;
Your answer is posted before I ask.
How I cherish knowing that You love to hear from me!
And, my Lord, how I wait impatiently for Your RSVP.

CHOICES

Ah, we think those sly, persuasive words,
"Had we but world enough, and time..."
And we believe our science—
OUR science, we call it, as if we invented it—
Can answer every *why* that crowds our mind and heart.
We dance at the cusp of bio-engineering
And all the power we think it represents,
Power to change what we think should not be
But we forget to consult with You to ask, "Mother, may I?"
Like our fatal choice in Paradise,
We spurn all that is freely given to take what is forbidden,
What is dangerous,
What we think we can handle
What we think we deserve.
Like the young child who observes how his parents drive,
Then takes the key,
Cranks, sparks, starts,
Presses forward—
Dangling feet barely able to reach,
Eyes unable to see what lies ahead,
Oblivious to the impending crash.

REFLECTORS

We see them everywhere:
Red mirrored discs that line rural drives
Like posies on steel stalks
Guarding the edges and hedges from wayward plows,
Deflecting drunks from those insidious ditches.
Holograms heralding dead ends, closed roads,
Washed out bridges or construction sites.
Reflectors on the fenders of trikes and bikes,
On helmets and jackets blading, boarding or scooting by.
Flashing eyes of wildlife at night, giving back borrowed light.

You call us, Lord, to reflect.
To absorb Your Light,
And to bounce it back for all to see,
A herald,
A warning,
A proclamation,
A sign.
Do what you will, only know:
God Almighty is present, at work among us.
And what an awesome eyeful You are, dear God!

ENCOMPASSED

I came early into the world, impatient and unfinished;
Without eyelashes or fingernails,
I left the womb unprotected but eager to go.
We are all unfinished,
Unprotected,
Unprepared,
Unfit for the journey,
Unqualified for the destination.
We are lost without You, Lord,
You are our first Parent,
Our Defense,
Our Outfitter,
Our Planner,
Our Map,
Our Passport,
Our Insurance against all risks.

February 4

PRAISE

Natural as breathing
Easy as a smile
Simple as hello
Regular as sunrise
Hallelujah is on my lips
Every moment, all my days
You alone are worthy of worship
You alone deserve such praise
Because Your grace is endless
Because Your mercies never cease
You are Lord of Creation
You are the Prince of Peace.

LIFELINES

Lord, thank You for trials
For accidents that stop us short
For illness that slows us from the daily blur
And forces us to focus again on You;
For frights and scares
That snap us back to the now and into Your waiting arms;
For near misses that cause us to ask What if
And bring us to our knees
Before You.
Thank You, Lord, for trials
So we can pray for each other
As You taught us
So we can ask for Your help
Your healing
Your blessing
Your mercy
Your grace
Your face.
Always
Your loving face.

February 6

THE GENUINE ARTICLE

Our teachers, scientists and philosophers
Implore us to take control of our lives
And to create our own destiny.
Our businessmen, politicians and economists
Persuade us to let them control our lives
For the better, of course,
So we can work out our own success.
Our parents tell us, in good faith,
We can be whatever we want to be.
Our doctors tell us good health and long life
Are matters of diet, exercise and good genes.

But it is You, God Almighty,
You who create our genes,
You who draw our life's journey,
You who define our success,
You who want to be Lord of our lives
So we can enjoy our true destiny.
We don't want to accept counterfeit joy,
Empty promises or dead ends.
We praise You!
We glorify You!
We ask for renewed faith,
To follow You wherever You lead.

GRIEVING

It seems impossible even as I say it, Lord,
But I thank You for mourning and grief.
Thank You for the passion that connects people:
The love that crafts friendship, fellowship, family;
The complex cloth loomed over time
Strand by strand
With meticulous care by Your Weaver's hand.
And when a strand is severed
Or a knot tied off
Thank You for allowing us the grace to weep
The ability to feel the anguish of loss
The freedom to shout our anger, our pain.
Thank You for taking our screams
Our pummeling fists
Our protests of injustice
Our pleas to reunite the broken threads.
Thank You for the process of grief.
It reminds us we are mortal
It reminds us we are interdependent
It reminds us we are unique
It reminds us that love is part ache...
It reminds us that You,
Creator of the universe,
Ransom for the lost,
Sanctifier of the sinful,
You weep;
You ache;
You grieve, too,
Whenever we break away.

BOUND UP

*They that wait upon the LORD shall renew their strength;
they shall mount up with wings as eagles.*—Isaiah 40:31

Thank You, dear God, for Your infinite patience,
Your eternal love, compassion and mercy.
Lord, You know what children we are.
We fight with each other over such folly;
We scream and holler, pull hair and pout;
We don't play nicely and we refuse to share.
We whine about every little bump along the way.
We always want to know if we're there yet.
Yet, impatient as we are to arrive,
We just have to stop,
Right now,
To poke around and probe each swamp,
Every thicket, and the occasional cave!
Then we wail for You to come find us,
To reach that strong arm in, that firm hand,
And save us from our own entanglement.

CARETAKERS

You have honored us with a trust
That we often mistake for burden
And try to throw off, or return.

Lord of heaven, infinite and eternal,
You have honored us with a trust:
We are tillers of Your garden,
Harvesters of Your plenty,
Wardens of Your wildlife,
Plumbers of Your wells.

Alpha and Omega, our all in all,
You have honored us with a trust:
To be stewards of Your stores,
Builders of Your temple, and—
In spite of Cain's guilty retort—
We are our brother's keeper.
We are bearers of one another's load.
We are bearers of Your standard.
We are bearers of Your cross.

DOORS

Give thanks to our Lord!
The gate of our sheepfold,
He knows where we stray;
He knows if we're in or out;
He keeps the wolves at bay.

Sing thanks to our Lord!
The carpenter who crafts the door,
Who frames and plumbs it true;
The lamb whose blood is shed
That no harm may come through.

Shout praise to our Lord!
He is the Door; He is the key;
He is the Word we must say.
No one may enter without Him.
He will make a way where there is no way.

JOY

Joy is a candle in the window
To draw us in from the dark.
Joy is a banner unfurled by hearts
To proclaim the King's presence.
Joy shared is a mosaic mural:
Each tessera a tiny broken shard,
But all united by the Master's hand
They illuminate and inspire awe.
Joy is the song of a lark,
Taken up by the wind,
Rustled through reeds,
And walked across my treble clef.

When grief grabs hold
Or despair bears down,
Joy comes in the morning.

You are my Light,
Monarch of the universe,
My soul's delight,
Engineer, Poet, Composer,
Joybringer.
Joygiver.
Pure joy.

HUNGER

Lord, You are my feast in the midst of famine.
You are my breakfast, lunch and dinner.
You are my midnight snack, my coffee break,
The taste I crave, the answer to my longing.
You still the grumblings of my mind,
You fill the cavernous belly of my soul.
I eat, I drink in remembrance of You.

CONTRACT

I mean it when I say it
I mean it when I pray it
But, like, sometimes life gets in my way.
I wanna walk da way ya call it
I wanna give ya my best, my all—yet
You & I know I'm bound to fall.

But ya took da fall for me.
Ya did da time. Ya died
'Cause 'a da contract on me.
I don't deserve ya, Lord!
I'm in awe of ya, Lord!
Ya did da time and died for me.

ROAD SIGNS

Yield. Stop. Dead End.
No through road.
Caution.
Under construction.
Every day we need direction
Every day we depend on signs…
Thanks to You, Mapmaker,
We can find the way.
Due to You, Master Engineer,
The road carries through.
Through You, dear Crossing Guard,
When we yield,
When ask You to put us
Under construction,
No power can stop us;
Our destination is sure.

WAITING

It's only fitting. You are the Lord,
Which makes me Your lady
In waiting.
Thank You for teaching me the wisdom
Of patience.
And its pain.
Thank You for showing me that doing
Is sometimes not.
Thank You for long moments of pause,
For suspended activity,
For time to stop the tick-tock pulse of life.
Thank You, Lord,
For freeing us from the tyranny of shoulds,
For arresting our daily rehearsal of oughts;
Thank You, Lord,
For allowing us to stop trampling
Essentials underfoot with the mundane;
For slowing our stampede
Until we tread gently enough to hear Your tender voice.
Thank You for the frustration of the waiting room,
Where we have only the old stories to read,
Yet where we see their truth,
Maybe for the first time.

WIRED

I don't need a degree in cybernetics
To do desktop publishing or to surf the web;
Someone else installs the PC
And its auxiliaries;
Someone else selects the software.
I download and blunder my way through,
With Dummy books, Help screens,
Support staff and friends.
But life is another matter entirely.
We are the hardware;
The programs came installed:
Bare bones, sure, but always upgradeable.
Some attractive add-ins eat memory;
And there's that insidious, innate virus
That corrupts our files and disrupts our drive.
Only You, Author of all knowledge,
Can scan, debug, defrag and reboot us
And only You can provide the Interface
To draw us from a seductive virtuality
Into infinite and eternal reality.

WEBS

Lord, the cosmos is filled with ironies
And curious juxtapositions.
Everyday banalities hide genius,
Invention and miracle.
Give us eyes to see, dear God,
And the wisdom to delight in Your world.

Ephemeral threads interconnect:
Their pattern is a safety net for some,
A jewel glistening with dew,
Yet a lethal trap for the spinner's meal.

Duck feet, awkward as snowshoes on dry land,
Become great props in the pool!

Weak strings break under tension,
But woven together they are flexible bands,
Meshed into strong support.

Instant global communication offers both revelation
And deception. Oh, what a tangled one we weave…

Your world is, like us, fearfully and wonderfully made;
We have the capacity to enjoy or destroy it.
Pull us into Your web, Lord; inform our choices
That we may be secure in Your strength,
Interlocked as servants of Your will.

QUESTIONS

It's confusing, Lord.
Some things are good for us,
While too much becomes poison.
Some things are poison to us,
Yet tiny portions can heal.
Some things are bad for us,
Though You have given them purpose.
Some things seem heaven for us,
But take us to the jaws of hell.
You made us curious—
We want to know all.
You gave us aspirations
And the desire to achieve.
Turn our vision outward, I pray,
That we may aspire to know You,
Desire to achieve Your will,
And want to become quite precisely
No more, no less
What You made us each to be.

CONTAGION

Giggles
Snickers
Titters
Chuckles
Chortles
Cheek puffers
Belly jostlers
Side-clutchers
Guffaws

Quiet or explosive
Sometimes soundless
Always infectious
Laughter is precious
Life-affirming
Miraculous
A great gift from You,
Clown of Clowns,
Master of Mirth,
To us children.
We begin by watching
But as we are drawn closer
By Your invitation
We become fully infected,
Jibed away from our dis-ease,
Dysfunction, disrespect and disuse,
Buoyed into action,
Keen to spread the joy.

FOCUS

Lord, we build cathedrals to Your glory.
We craft spectacular pipe organs
To accompany our worship.
We cast huge bells and create carillons
To ring out Your praise.
We dress our children and ourselves
To come before our King.

But You dressed Yourself in simplicity.
You came and left with little fanfare.
A pebble in the ocean,
You set off a slow tsunami
That is still shaking us from our moorings.
Hallelujah!

ONE WINTER MORNING

Precious Creator,
Thank You for frosty crystals on the grass
And icy glaze on the forest.
Thank You for the way sunlight sparkles
And prisms through the icicles on the eaves
And fingers down from the snow-laden clouds.
Thank You for my white breath on the invisible air
A marker, for the moment, that I am living in this space.
A reminder, for the moment, that Your Spirit,
Your Breath, is living here within me
And without
Abroad in this fallen world
Your ancient and future paradise.

TALENT

How particularly You have graced some people, dear God!
What remarkable artists have blessed our lives!
Ears that hear grass burst from its seed;
Ears that hear the hum of electrons spinning;
Eyes that see within, behind, before…in spite of;
Eyes that see nothing as mundane;
Hands that translate epiphany and revelation
Into common language for ordinary senses.
These special prophets ferry us
Across the torrents of blasé disregard,
Beyond the rocks of human thou shalt nots,
To the paradise of illumination.

BLESSINGS

As letters gather up to create words,
As words gather in lines to create images,
As images gather on a page to express insights,
Your blessings are the text of our lives—
How often, alas, we forget our reading glasses.

As dew rolls glistening down blades of grass
As rain steps gently down from leaf to leaf,
As streams feed through rivers to the sea,
Your blessings often pass unnoticed,
Like scattered impressions, gone too soon.

Like chicks in the nest, we squawk
Raucously, mouths wide open,
Protesting our imperative need.
Forgive us, Lord, for being oblivious
While You lovingly feed us Yourself.

LONGING

Lord, we decorate our spaces.
We bring the outdoors in
And take the indoors out.
We want to make ourselves an Eden
In the midst of worldly decay.

We dream of Paradise
Where we are clothed in purity,
Fed with the Bread of Life,
Slaked with Living Water,
Protected by our Rock and our Shelter,
And loved,
Always
Loved.

We ache for the original Garden,
But like our arch-ancestors,
We want to be the gardeners,
Not the rootstock.

CAPSTONE

As You know so well, dear Lord,
My life is built of many things.
There are sticks and stones:
Some gathered, some thrown.
There is concrete, there is mud,
There is paper. There's Your blood.
Many hands have helped to heap
Such incongruous materials into strong walls;
Many hands have helped to sweep
Away unwanted debris and wash the halls
Clear of toxic waste. Precious Redeemer,
Of all that is lasting, resilient and admired
Of all the blocks, bricks and stones,
You alone, my Rock, are corner, key and cap.

A ROUND

Lord, there is mud underfoot
But cerulean sky overhead!
There is still snow on the lawn
But cardinals dot the hollies, bright as berries!
There are dead trees and windbroken boughs,
But bulbs will soon release their blooms!
There are forlorn folks, winter-sick
But soon they will be joyfilled, Easter-healed.
Thank You, loving, gracious God:
You always give us handholds of hope.

LOOK UP

We look to the heavens so often,
Yet too frequently forget to praise their Maker.
We check the weather, overhead and on the horizon;
We consult the stars, for either science or fiction;
We test the winds, for pleasure or safe measure;
We linger at sunrise and sunset,
We recreate them on film or in oils;
We admire scattered beams of sunlight
Breaking through pewter clouds,
Like fingers of blessing over gilded cities.
We speak poetically of the canopy of stars,
Forgetting our Tentmaker and Kindler of Lights.
Accept this praise, Almighty Eternal One,
Accept this praise, these thanks, this awe.

CHAPEL

Great joy!
Near perfect exuberant, exultant joy!
The communion of saints and Spirit
Around words of praise
Thanksgiving
And worship.
Great joy, dear Lord,
As You are elevated,
Celebrated,
Adored.
Love shared builds a cathedral
Rising on alleluias and amens…
Until
One
Angry
Word
Shatters the rising chord
Scowling into minor key.
Renew our love, I pray,
Heal this intruding pain
Unsplinter the rash discord
Help us recover our harmony
And resolve from dark to light.

LEAP DAY

Got my shoes on, Lord, and ready to jump!
Leap, holler, spin and dance
Today's more than a second chance
Today's made for balance, to scoop up
Those extra quarter days we threw out
Three years running... now we score
An extra inning, overtime, home free!
So I got my shoes on, Lord,
My cushy rubber soles, sneaks, tennies,
B-ball walking jogging running
Cross-training boat and dancing shoes,
I'm ready to rock and roll,
Hop, jump, bound, soar,
Leap for joy! Thank you, Lord,
For surprises round the bases
All the way home.

EMPTY?

One slice of bread
Last drop of juice
Zero oranges
No milk
Breakfast on the fly
Vacant roads—don't know why
Needle nearly on E—gotta stop now
Gotta get going
Jot a note
Remember to shop
Research and write that paper
Read those books
Don't forget the meeting tonight…
And with my load
I'm thinking
I could be running on empty, too…
Except for You.
No matter what I need
No matter when
Even if I haven't yet asked
You know. You care. You love.
You fill my cup to overflowing
And You restore my soul.
I'll never be empty again.

ASHES

We think of them as charred remains
Relics of what was but is no more—
The fragile, nearly ephemeral, result
Of great and violent destruction.
Ashen is a negative word,
A lack of color, a loss of vitality:
Wan, gaunt, reduced, burnt up…
But ashes are fertile, fecund:
Both funeral pyre and womb.
Certain endings are required
To render possible true beginnings.
Yesterday Your people celebrated
With the solemn ashes of discarded palms,
The start of the journey to the cross.
Thank You, precious Alpha AND Omega,
For teaching me that we must die to the world
Before we can rise up and truly live.

March 3

PASSION

Paintings. Portraits. Milkmaid or magnate.
Landscapes. Still life. Inward look or outward desire.
Etchings, engravings, sketches, pastels,
Any scrap and any marker will do
To retain three dimensions in two.
You have given us the gift to depict, to express;
You have filled us with unquenchable fire,
With stories to tell,
With hearts that swell
With recognition when we see,
Understand,
Dare to share the dream.

NAMES

We have many names for each other.
Some are formal, to show respect.
Some are friendly, an invitation,
An open door.
Some are, like passwords,
Reserved for the special few
Allowed beyond the veil of intimacy.
Handles, monikers, appellations—
We even have names for names!
We have hundreds of names for You:
Some are fancy, some plain;
Some are titles, to mark our esteem;
Yet others show relationship,
And how we are kin.
But You, Prince of Peace,
You are the name above all names,
The name at which,
One day, glorious day,
Every knee shall bow.

CURTAINS

We use them to protect our homes
To ward off an unwanted chill
To guard against prying eyes
To filter the warm but bleaching rays.
We hang them to decorate our space,
To coordinate color, texture, interest...
We curtain off hospital beds and dressing rooms;
We raise the curtain onstage or bring it down;
"Curtains for You" means someone's sure demise.
When Your Temple stood in Jerusalem,
There was a curtain of separation
Between Your holiness and our sins.
But when Jesus of Nazareth died on the cross,
Assuming all our guilt on his blameless back,
The curtain was ripped wide open
And, like sunlight after endless rain,
We were invited in, beyond the veil,
Where we could not step before.

March 6

HATS & GLOVES

I put on my warmest hat and gloves today
To clear snow and to haul wood inside—
Last night was just the leading edge
Of a record-challenging blizzard,
Or so they said,
And with each stroke of the shovel
I felt I was preparing the way,
Inviting a blanket of white to snug in
When in cold truth I'd like to torch it all
And get on with spring.
When I came inside,
Wet and pierced by the icy wind,
I began to reflect:
I have several hats and assorted gloves
That warm and protect me as best they can;
But I have only one coat, one hat,
One set of boots, one pair of gloves
That provide all the shelter I need—
In all places, all times, all weather,
Lord, I put You on first.
You are not always stylish in this world,
But let the fashion police mount their attack;
My Lord Immanuel covers me, head and hands,
And my feet will always walk the path He clears.

March 7

HELP

The snow,
Though less than foretold,
Stood as a wall
Between my car and the world.
Obligations pressing,
I struck out, shovel in hand,
Determination on my brow
And prayers for fortitude on my lips.
With vigor and hope,
I set about the daunting task.
Scrape, shape, lift and throw
Too soon became, however,
Scrape, shape, shove or drag.
And as I began to rest more
After clearing less,
I saw the solid fortress that remained
Like the rising hulk of Goliath.
My shovel seemed a puny weapon
Against this challenge,
And, as the deer pants after water,
I pleaded, "Lord???!"
And look! What joy!
As my David immediately appeared,
A mere boy wielding a plastic shovel,
Yet fearless before the formidable task.
This was no accident of fate, no happenstance.
My faith grows bolder every moment,
Because my help is always in the Lord.

March 8

FORETASTE

Today was a tantalizing taste
Of spring yet to come
A tease after three days of winter's worst
A glimpse of blue. And green. And robin's red.
A temptation to turn off the heat
And throw open the sash…
To listen in as rehearsal begins.
This is but a foretaste of future joy,
A reminder to see us through
When,
With renewed power,
The windblown snow
Returns.
These are windows of true joy, Lord,
Prequels to our eternal home
Where we began and where You await our return;
Glimpse of glory
Hints of heaven
A drum roll……
So let me be all ears, Lord,
Ready for Your complete symphony
Whenever You raise the baton.

WRITTEN IN STONE?

In memory of Santee & Williamsport

We teach our children to covet
We teach our children to steal
We teach our children to dishonor and to disrespect.
We teach our children to lie
We teach our children to cheat
We teach our children to judge looks, not character
We teach our children God is dead
And we teach our children to kill
Randomly
Theatrically
Dispassionately
Because they understand life has no value
And television is truth.

TRUST

We place our trust in government, Lord,
And forget that we are the people who govern.
We place our trust in casual friends, Lord,
Before we learn the true nature of their hearts.
We place our trust in lovers and open heart and home, Lord,
But some turn out to be cruel, relentless abusers.
We place our trust in banks, insurance companies, healthcare providers
Only to find them filling their pockets and ignoring our pain
Until they themselves are swallowed up by larger sharks.
We place our trust in technologies we don't understand
Sending our precious thoughts into electronic files
That sometimes crash or corrupt, leaving us empty.
Lord, we pull back,
Angry.
Betrayed.
Feeling duped and naïve,
We fold up and inward,
Trusting only ourselves...if that.
Lord, be our trust.
Give us back the assurance we need,
The faith that Your love is limitless, gracious, merciful,
And poured out for all of us.
Heal our wounds.
Give us hope.
Teach us to trust anew.

March 11

DUST

Tiny
Particles
Insidious
Ever-present
Exponentially
Accumulating
Invisibly suspended in air
Until revealed in the Light;
Appearing on every surface,
Layering until all color has gone grey.
How easy it is to ignore this film, this residue.
How like sin, my God, is this inexorable invasion.
Wipe us clean, Lord.
Renew our shine.

HANDS

Lord, what a privilege we have!
To lay loving hands on others
As we invoke Your blessing
And intercede for healing.
What a joy, Lord, to let our hands
Represent Yours
As we clasp each other's
In a circle of prayer,
And as we grasp shoulders
With comfort and tender warmth,
Or touch heads,
Anointing them with love.
Hands can so easily be used for ill,
Precious God,
But You have formed them to give
More than to take,
To hold up to heaven for mercy,
Not to hold down.
Your hands were pierced
And bled for us
So our hands could be free,
Ready to do Your work.

BELONGING

There's safety in numbers,
We tell ourselves.
That's why we like tour buses
Cruise ships
Tailgate parties and barbecues
Mahjong clubs
Exercise classes
Even group excursions to the loo.
We like to belong
But sometimes, my God,
We join blindly,
And like lemmings, or swine,
We find ourselves pouring into the flood.
Sometimes, Lord, we'd rather join up,
Wear the badge, the hat, the uniform,
The brown shirt or crooked cross,
To march in step so we don't stand out…
Protect us, dear Shepherd,
From the goats who lead us astray.
Open our eyes before it's too late.
Help us make discerning choices.
Knock on our hearts until we let You in,
That You may be the gatekeeper of our souls,
Our guide in this world and the next.

SIGNS OF SPRING

(New Brunswick Theological Seminary & Rutgers University intersect)

Eternal Lifebringer,
There is heart-stopping joy
In the tiny shoots of plum and white
Standing jubilantly, soldier straight,
Above the close-cropped carpet of lawn,
And in the purple clusters
That dot the dense ivy embankment.
We look up in gratitude, where
Leaves appear, tightly wrapped at treetips.
Your inexpressibly glorious Easter gift
Of life renewed
Is
Alas
Almost crowded out
Almost shouted down
By the distracting visual noise
Of discarded BK boxes, candy wrappers,
Plastic bags, broken pens, mail half-read,
The thoughtless refuse of the walking dead.
Lord, scatter burgeoning crocuses
In the path of these blind youths;
Open their eyes, reclaim their hearts,
Lest they, too, become litter along the way.

NOT QUITE SPRING

Thank You, God of peace,
For spring in winter
For sunshine through rain
For leisure amid strife
Warm welcome among strangers
Thank You for rest
When there is yet so much to do
For spices to spark taste from bland
For cold water, hot tea, lemon zest
For the joy of worship
And the privilege of chatting with You.

FRIDAY PRAISE

Praise to You, Almighty,
For children's laughter
Crashing through the wall.
Praise to You, my Lord,
For happy puppies
Wiggling down the hall.
Praise to You, Eternal One,
For March's mighty winds
And sun-bleached skies.
Praise to You, great Architect,
For spring's refreshing rains
To make our gardens rise.
Praise to You, Judge and Defender,
For providing a loophole
In Your own immutable, sacred law.
Praise to You, Lamb of God,
For the sacrifice of that Friday
So Sunday's glory could come to us all.

March 17

GREEN PEACE

It doesn't matter if he really threw out the snakes
It doesn't matter that he wasn't truly Irish at all
It doesn't matter whether he performed miracles
Every God-fearin' Christian is a saint.
It doesn't matter whether we drink green beer
It doesn't matter if we eat corned beef & cabbage or kale
It doesn't matter if we parade and sing *Danny Boy*
Every God-fearin' Christian is a saint.
And let no one curse me for speakin' plain
It doesn't matter whether orange or green we wear
It doesn't matter which altar feeds us
Or whether the cross there is bearin' or bare
Every God-fearin' Christian is a saint.
It doesn't matter who shot first
It doesn't matter who shot last
What matters is to put an end to murder
In—God forgive us!—Christ's name;
His blood was already spilt for all
And EVERY God-fearin' Christian is a saint.

JAZZ

For so many of us,
The alarm rudely starts the day
It sets the heart racing,
Hands and feet rushing about,
Sometimes in concert, sometimes not,
While the mind is still cobwebbed with dreams.
Teeth, gargle, hair, shower, powder, shave?
Dress, duty, feed the cat, routine,
Walk the dog, kiss the kid, run…
Start the car, grab that coffee, go.
Where do we squeeze You in, Lord?
A quick grumble as we silence the clock?
A howdy-let's-have-a-good-one as we lather up?
A thanks-for-the-grub as we gulp our Big Joe,
Burning rubber and a few sedate sedans
Along the way?
You give us infinite love, we wave hi.
You give us full attention, we pass You by.
You gave Your life for us, we give You a dime.
You offer eternity in Paradise, we can't find the time.

TRACKS

Footprints come and footprints go.
We assume they run heel to toe.
But people sometimes backwards walk,
Or more likely in wide circles, like talk—
Either way, they end up where they began
Scratching heads and throwing up hands.

Like these wanderers in the snow,
We don't like to admit that we're lost.
What fools we are! Ego is the only cost.
Why don't we ask You to guide us home?

CONNECTIONS

Levers move
Teeth mesh
Gears turn
Shafts spin
Wheels roll
Work is done.

Heart hurts
Eyes tear
Hands fold
Words form
Prayers rise
God hears
Love pours down.

EVENING CHAPEL

As I run the rapids of my life,
Sometimes the rocks loom perilously close.
Chapel channels into a placid pool,
Soothing
Cool
Smooth
Amid the rough assaults of wild edges.

As I run down and begin to fade,
A mere fifteen hours into the day,
Chapel rouses me
Stimulating
Invigorating
Rejuvenating
So I can give three more hours of my best.

Just as I am feeling unraveled
By unrelenting concerns and demands,
Chapel renews me:
Restful
Reflective
Restorative
Living Water for parched lips.
Hallelujah!

A NEW SONG

I have my limited range of songs and
Sometimes I'm afraid You'll get bored;
I have a dozen or so favorite tunes
That seem to stick in my head, Lord;
I'd like to think You put them there
Because You enjoy them, too.
When I want to sing Your praise,
I recycle words, get stuck at the start,
But when I have no new songs to raise
You hear my thoughts, You read my heart.
You fill my cup, You give me everything I have…
You wake me, walk with me, and You close my day.
My greatest joy is in Your presence, God.
You made me who I am, You light my way.

ROAD TO HEALTH

Cherished Lord,
You are my source *and* my destination.
You are the path I walk.
You are the Word *and* the Poem.
You are my breath.
You are the health of my heart:
While You excise the clots, the plaque,
All that obstructs, hinders or restricts,
Your touch heals old scars, regenerating with love.
As You drain out my blood, infected with sin,
You transfuse it with Christ's own, holy and clean.

CLOUDS

Lord, what a sky this morning!
Crammed with clouds:
Rolling thunderheads,
Asphalt grey,
Layered and packed tight,
So heavy with storm
They drag against the road,
Frowning, furious, furrowed
On the horizon;
Sandwiched in are rows
Of less menacing water bearers,
Like cows with sagging bellies
They bounce and sway
In the wind;
Periodically there are banks
Of white batting, brilliant
Where Your glory pokes through
And pours down on us.
I wish, my Lord, that I could paint,
Brushing water colors on a textured,
Wet, white page,
Where the smoky wisps
Would take shape.
I would need an infinite palette:
Every possible shade of grey,
Unnoticed subtleties of white,
Echoes and intimations of blue,
Flicks of red, rose, russet and ruby...
Yet it would still be limited, Lord,
To the borders of the page
And the boundaries of human skill.
Thank You, gracious God,
For this spectacular vision to start this day.
Your boundless blessings are breathtaking.

March 25

BOOKS

At home, at school, at work,
I am surrounded by books
As diverse in size, shape and color
As the people who wrote and read them.
Filled with mystery, love, adventure,
Travel, poetry, paintings & sculptures,
Spies, space, science…
Questions. Answers to questions.
Human words, pages of words
That transport and entrance me.
In my library, there are several languages;
Some I swig like cold water on a dusty day,
While deciphering a few is a brow-knitting task.
Thank You, Lord, for giving us words,
Especially the words that connect us,
That make us realize again and again
All people are a community, bound together
By dreams, by fears, by what is common,
By what is not;
By Your love,
Which is both common and unique.

BOOKMARKS

They accumulate in readers' lives:
Colored ribbons, cardboard slivers,
Pewter blades, flat plastic critters,
Rectangles of leather, maybe embossed,
Some with fringe, some squared off.
They are decorated with drawings,
Photos, quotations. Or not.
Sometimes we reach instead for a string,
A paper clip,
A scrap sheet…
Anything to avoid dog-earring the page
Of the precious book.
Bookmarks mark our page for us,
They hold our place until we return,
They preserve the pleasure of diving back in
Without hunting for that same delightful spot.
Bookmarks mark our place.
There is one book that marks our lives
By showing us where we are
And where we are going;
Where and who we have been,
Who we are called to be.
Your book, Lord, marks our place
In Your plan for all creation.
Your book has a start and a finish,
Yet we can open anywhere to hear You speak.
Thank You, Lord, for the book that marks every generation,
The book that calls us home to You.

March 27

SHOUT

Can it be, Lord, that I have no praise today?
All day I searched for Newness,
But today's rebirth is winter
And, forgive my petulance, God,
But I can't praise this step back.
I'm thinking of warm fronds
And joyful hallelujahs
Weaving and waving
Through the sun-charged air.
My heart is set on Easter's glory
And I don't want to walk the path
Of cold stones
Of turned backs and raised fists
Of whips and thorns,
Of hammerstrokes ringing out
Against ice-sharp nails,
Of torture, abandon, hypocrisy, lies
All pinning the King of the Universe
To a tree on the skull-like hill.
I don't want to admit
That winter's discomfort and destruction
Make the miracle of spring a reality.
The grain of corn must drop to the ground and die…
Everything has a purpose
And every purpose has a time.
You are Life, my Lord.
You are the Overcomer and Renewer.
You have all my praise,
Whispered today,
Tomorrow in shouts!

DEATHWATCH

For Sebastian

Perhaps more than at any other time, great God,
I am reminded,
As the angel of Death hovers over my beloved
But tarries
And as I tend to his final comforts,
How sweetly You minister to us,
Performing all the same acts of love:
How completely You envelop us with Your arms,
How You warm our aged bodies so gently
To avoid crushing our bones, now brittle.
How You offer water to our parched lips,
Living Water to our thirsty souls—
Prisoners within the ribs of our sunken cell,
Nomads struck down by a cold desert wind.
How You speak the sweet promise of peace.
How You touch us, renewing our special bond,
And rekindling in us the first flames of joy...
We are only sojourners here.
Let my beloved enter Your gates, I pray,
That he may leap up into Your waiting arms.

LEAVE-TAKING

In memoriam: Sebastian

So many times these past weeks
I told him he could go, Lord,
And how persistently I asked You,
Every day
Every night;
I begged You to take him home.
But Lord this morning
What agony
As I scooped him up
Carried him aimlessly
About the house
On outstretched arms
Like a little girl
With a worn-out rag doll.
I cradled him
And clasped him to my breast
This beloved child of my heart,
As though holding him close
Might slow the separation
And dull the pain of absence.
You wept for Lazarus, Lord,
As You wept over Jerusalem.
Weep now with me.

CARE

What a privilege it is, Lord,
To tend to each other,
To be Your hands in the world.
It is a blessing to share sorrow,
To hug away a portion of pain.
It is an honor to be Your second, Lord,
To listen to someone else's woe,
To witness another's life trials,
To comfort and console.
It is a mercy to wipe away tears,
To rediscover the great healing
In the gentle touch of a hand.
But sometimes we forget
In our moments of anguish or grief
To allow others the privilege
Of caring for us.
Thank You, Ancient of Days,
For breaking my pride and
For sending so many to tend to me.

LIGHTS

On the roads this morning,
Through the fog, the floods,
So many drivers were speeding along
With no headlights
Despite the downpour.
The dark.
And I began to realize, Lord,
How often we careen through life
Sure we know where we're going,
Certain we see clearly how,
Convinced we are in perfect control,
Yet we are not only blind
And stumbling in the dark,
But we are also dangerous obstacles
To others following along
Who may not see us in their way.
Like those who don't know they need glasses
Until they look through the proper lens,
We need lights, Lord;
We need Your Light
To clear the path before us
To shine out from within us
To be a beacon to others
Who are still in the dark.

JOYS

There are many flavors of joy, Lord.
Today's was the delight of speaking Your word;
Seeing so many faces, earnest and intent,
Eager to listen;
Realizing that suddenly there was no restlessness,
No coughing or rustling of paper,
No shuffling of feet;
Hearing an exuberant basso profundo
Shout AMEN! from the back pews.
Joy today was being a fool for Christ in Warwick, New York.

SPECIAL DAYS

Some days have extra value;
We turn the calendar page
And suddenly the videos start,
The photo album flips open,
And, unbidden, the memories fan out—
Birthday, wedding, graduation,
First date, new job, joyful starts…
Funeral, divorce, downsizing,
Failed business, departure, life up-ended…
We commemorate—we remember together
The events that shape our days.
Thank You, Lord,
For giving us the desire to celebrate
And commiserate,
For giving us the need to share
Ups and downs,
Joys and sorrows,
Special days:
What we want to remember;
What we can't forget.
Thank You for giving us community.

COLORS

What a rich palette You have given us, Lord,
To paint our holidays and seasons.
Spring is bright green with promise,
Pink and lilac and yellow with proliferating blooms.
Summer is rich in light, bright, full blues of sky and ocean.
Autumn is pumpkin, cranberry, pinecone and mustard.
Winter is snow and mud; bright stars and fog.
Christmas is green and red, bedecked with gold,
Blue and silver tell us Hanukkah is here.
Purple is Lent; a time of royalty, a time of penitence,
A time of approaching grief.
Easter is white, lilies and angel wings and an empty tomb.
The purity of rebirth.
The colorlessness of Holy God.

AGAPE OF CHRIST

There is no other word to name it,
Lord Christ;
We can only draw on adjectives
To describe Your love
As brotherly, motherly;
Sacrificial, other-oriented,
Unselfish, unlimited,
Forgiving, transforming,
Illuminating, encouraging, comforting,
Unexpected, extra-ordinary, super-natural;
Uncontrolling yet disciplinary;
Unimposed yet discipling,
Surrendering,
Ever-unfolding,
Eternal, immeasurable love.
Agape of Christ.
Let my love emulate and approximate
As far as You can take my heart.

RECEIVING

Thank You, merciful God,
Wellspring of all blessings,
For the spontaneous generosity of others;
For giving us opportunities to learn
Not just the immense joy of giving,
But also the grace to gratefully accept
A wholly unmerited gift.

MUSIC

There are people who write music
Because Your Spirit sings to them in dreams,
At the marketplace, along the road…
There are people who make music
Because You confer upon them talent. Skill.
And fire in the belly to lift the notes from the page.
There are people who conduct the music
Because You give them vision. And passion.
And eloquence of limb,
To lead, coax, drive, direct,
Diminuendo, ritardando or *crescendo*,
To quell or swell the resonance of our hearts.

WHISPERS

You are my peace
You are my calm
You are Lord God
Holding me in Your palm
You love my laugh
You dry my tears
Soothe my heartcry
And defang my fears
You watch my back
You smoothe my hair
You save me from myself
You have made me Your heir.

WATER

As essential as air
As exquisite as gemstone when You bring on the lights
As compelling and as fearsome as the greatest beast
It is our world's dominant feature
It is our body's major component
It appears on the ground overnight like manna
It falls from heaven, be it blessing or curse
It is fuel
It is fun
It is fire-quenching
It is flood
It is transport
It is transfixing
It is trammeling
It is trying
It is, like You who made it, dear Lord,
Too often taken for granted.

RETREAT

Glory to You, Almighty God, for gentle mornings,
Mist in the garden and scurrying squirrels;
Nuthatches and finches under the window
Raising songs of praise.
Glory to You, Holy God, for places of retreat
From the press and stress that roll us out like dough
Then raise the heat that we may feed many.
Glory to You, Creator God, for peaceful hills
Agèd orchards and fragrant spring soil;
For respite, release from the wrinkles of life.

THE LAMB

Today is Pesach and Palm Sunday.
Today we celebrate with joyful praise
Today we shout Hosanna! Hallelujah!
Today we follow the time-honored rituals
Today we retell the ancient stories
Today we kindle flames of thanksgiving
Today we recite prayers of old
Today we remember the journey
Today we rejoice
Today we are redeemed
Today we remember the Paschal Lamb
Today we worship You, precious Lord,
For You delivered us with two outstretched arms.

A LITANY OF THANKS

Thank You for Your watchful eye
Thank You for Your guiding hand
Thank You for Your warning voice
Thank You for Your protective care
Thank You for Your sheltering arm
Thank You for Your shepherd's staff
Thank You for Your ageless word
Thank You for Your unending grace

MAUNDY THURSDAY

Lord, teach us tonight to wash each other's feet
At the table of grace
Teach us tonight to break bread together
At the table of peace
Teach us tonight to drink from the same glass
At the table of sacrifice
Lord, teach us tonight to pray wakefully
In the garden of solitude
Teach us tonight to forgive one another
In the garden of betrayal
Teach us tonight to stand, quietly united in purpose
In the garden of mob justice
Teach us tonight to profess our faith
Beside the fires of inquisition
Lord, teach us tonight to be steadfastly Yours
When the world says no.
Teach us tonight to wait patiently for answers,
To use Your gifts with wisdom and love,
To trust You for healing and comfort,
And to be Your good and faithful servants
In the upper rooms, the Gethsemanes
And the Calvaries of our lives.

FRIDAY THE 13TH

It is Good Friday again,
The day when the incorruptible became sin
The day when the Eternal suffered and died
The day when man's evil was used for man's good.
Today we remember.
Today we acknowledge
That we would have cried out, "Crucify him!"
Instead of weeping with the women.
We would have shrugged defensively,
Saying, like Peter, "Not me, I don't know him!"
Instead of proclaiming, "Yes, I am his!"
Today we light candles,
Then one by one blow them out,
And silently go home to grieve.
How sad that it is often our own sins we mourn.

LITTLE PLEASURES

A stranger's nod
A toddler's smile
A dog's playful leap
A butterfly on the gentle wind
Thank You for simple joys
Fresh-mown grass
Just peeled oranges
Fragrant roses
Blocks of cedar
Thank You for smells to savor
Garden chimes
Giggles and guffaws
Gurgling water
Sparrows singing spring
Thanks for spontaneous music
You surround us, Lord,
With limitless little pleasures
To tickle our senses
And bring our attention back to You.

April 15

TIME OFF

Sometimes we just need to do nothing.
Sometimes we need to sleep, rest, dream.
Sometimes we need to go fishing,
Read a book, do some knitting,
Paint a sunset, write a poem.
Thank You for the Sabbath day
And Your command to rest
As You did
After Your busy week
Of creating the universe and all that lives.
Our spheres of influence are smaller, Lord,
But we are thankful for the work and the play.

THE IDES

Some say, beware the Ides of April—
It's that loathsome Tax Day in America.
But for the world it's Resurrection Day!
Glory be to You, O God,
For the miracle of Easter,
The promise of new life,
Around us and within us,
The realization that redemption is at hand.
We are assured of eternity with You;
The door to Your Kingdom is open,
And we are joint heirs to the throne.

FLAWS

Sometimes carpenters hammer their thumbs.
Sometimes even divas sing off key.
Sometimes engineers miscalculate.
Sometimes architects misalign.
Sometimes pilots rock and roll.
Sometimes actors miss a line.
Sometimes teachers have no answer.
We are so demanding.
We are so ungracious.
We are so unforgiving.
We forget.
We forget.
We forget.
Only one human ever was perfect
And You are God.

WINDOWS

Everyone knows
Windows are opportunities
Openings from one space to another
Passageways through boundaries
Portals for visions
And dreams.
They are also filters
Transitions
Protected looks
Low risk ways to consider
Possibilities.
They open, they close;
They slide, they pop.
They're tinted or clear;
Draped. Or blinded. Or not.
Triple-paned storms
Or fine-meshed screens,
They keep the bugs
And the bugaboos
Out.
They keep the heat
And the cool
In.
But sometimes
What is in needs to get out
And what is out needs to get in.
Lord, make me a window to You.

April 19

FISHBOWL

Sitting in the diner
I hear how people brag
Or gossip
Or advise—
With more concern for looking smart,
Powerful,
Than truly counseling their tablemates.
The servers kiss up or slam down.
The hostess glowers at waiting guests
With open hostility
Because they intrude upon her conversation.
Besides, it's a busy day
And Papa is away.
Behind me, the busboy sounds as though
He is breaking as many dishes as he can
And I think this is how You see us every day:
Angry, petulant, impatient,
Uncaring, self-important, self-righteous,
Blaring our own horns
In the now-deaf ear of others.
Yet You love every one of us, Lord,
As only a parent can:
Every foolish, obnoxious, boastful, striving one of us.

PICNIC

I want to stretch out a checkered cloth
Under a massive oak somewhere sunny,
Lay out knives, forks and spoons—
Ready to cut, separate, dip into this feast
You have prepared.
But I would hardly know
Which thing to do first!
Clamber up into the wide branches
Where I want to be but am afraid to go,
To swing my legs in the fresh currents
Of Your gentle breath?
Or unpack the hamper of Your Word,
Unfolding the pages,
Pondering the verses,
Chewing thoughtfully, prayerfully,
On the succulent lessons,
Enjoying the texture of the difficult bits,
Letting Your fragrant whispers linger.

There is still snow on the ground, Lord,
But You have brought me sun enough.

MUSEUMS

Museums are churches
Where the poor in spirit come to find God
Reflected in human creation.

THE SEASON OF SINGING

"Flowers appear on the earth; the season of singing has come."
Song of Solomon 2:12

And sing I must, Almighty One,
Not like the birds, for my voice is other
Though my joy be greater than a flock's;
Not like the ocean, for my wind is weak
And drowned by the percussive tide;
Not like the clouds, for my lightest notes fall earthward
To tinkle against the rocks, while the billows breeze on;
Not like the wildflowers sown by passing creatures
And the occasional wind, for my song is mute
Against the colors and shapes of Your simplest garden.
Yet sing I must, Almighty One,
Your praise and Your glory!
With every breath,
Every beat of my heart,
Every glance of my eye,
I sing Your holiness, Your mercy, Your grace, Your love.

THANKS

Thank You is such a pedestrian phrase,
Such an everyday platitude
It seems unfitting for the Ruler of the Universe
It seems too plain for the Giver of all Gifts
It seems inadequate for the Ancient of Days
But it's the best I have, my Rock and my Redeemer,
To show my ceaseless gratitude.
Thank You.

FORSYTHIA

Although pastel pinks, lavenders, pale blues and tender greens
Usually are Spring's transition from the dreary deadness of winter
I suddenly noticed this morning, Creator,
That You break through the lifeless browns and muddy greys
With spectacular splashes of shimmering yellow
Sensational
Inescapable
Sun-drenched
Brilliant yellow
Crocus
Jonquil
Daffodil
Dandelion
They stand straight, as single sentries
Or gathered groups ready for Reveille.
They blanket fields and knolls like shafts of sun.
But the greatest sunburst of all, dear Lord, is Your forsythia:
Each untamed hedge of splayed branches
Disheveled like a punk hairdo
And alive, exploding, with bright blooms.

April 25

WHEN OUR CHILDREN DIE

In memoriam: Jessica

It's a tragedy, Lord, when our children die
Time is upside down and life is inside out
Nothing makes sense anymore
We seethe and grieve and beat our breast
We kick walls, hurl insults at objects,
We scream out to You in indignant despair,
"How could You take her?!"
"He was so young!"
"Why didn't You take me first? It's not supposed to work this way!"
And like children ourselves we tell You You're unfair
This death is premature
Yet it is we who must adjust our clocks
Because Your timing is always perfect.
We muster our faith, so fragile in our pain,
To tell ourselves we should rejoice
To know the child is safe in Your arms again,
Spared the hideous anguish of this world
That we have refashioned,
Where other children are shooting one another
Or shooting craps, or shooting up.
Thank You, Lord, yes even for this tragic loss
Because we know You are in control.
You will provide comfort, and healing, and hope.
You know what it's like.
After all, Your child died young, too.

CURSES

Lord, You have told us that those whom we curse
You will curse
And those whom we bless
You will bless.
Forgive me, almighty merciful God,
For the days I want You to curse so many!
I want You to visit on them the evils they do
I want You to show them they have no power
To strip them of their arrogant audacity
To send locusts to eat their idols
To have others do unto them as they did unto us
To crash their computers and their stocks
To seize a piston in their monster trucks
To put undisciplined obnoxious brats in their face
(Yes, of course, I mean someone else's)
To unleash recklessly cruel bullies on them…
Forgive me, I pray, lest my curses implode on me.

LESSONS OF THE WRAP

Lord, it's lunchtime
And I am grateful
For the zest of mustard
That, like any great joy,
Raises gooseflesh and drops tears.
Spice is enhancement
And preservation; I remember
You call us to be the salt of the earth.

I am grateful
For the fresh, earthy crunch
Of shredded lettuce
And the slippery, sweet squish
Of tomato reminding me
That when people recognize my faith
It is due to fruits of Your Spirit.

I am even grateful
For the messy juice that drips
From the wrap wrongly bitten
Because it reminds me
I am bathed in Your blessings
And washed by Your grace.

April 28

ROCKS

Each one is unique
Irregular or standard
Crooked or straight
Smooth-cheeked or pock-marked
Some march in order,
Fashioning a lintel or an arch;
Most are heaped together
Working shoulder to hip,
Bearing each other up
For foundation, walls and tower.
Some are helped into shape
But most come as they are, flaws and all.
The result is massive
Strong
Solid
United
Majestic
Natural beauty employed by human hands
To create a sanctuary
From the pains of outside
And for communion inside
With the One who shapes us.

QUALITY OF LIGHT

I'm no scientist, Lord,
To determine the angle of sun to horizon,
Or the filtering effects of spatial debris,
Of atmospheric humidity and pollution,
The g-force of other cosmic bodies,
Or the latitude and longitude on our globe;
But I have noticed that there is a quality of light
At certain times of day
At certain times of year
At certain locations I have been
That is so exquisite,
So pregnant with hue,
So eye-pleasing and heart-filling
So fleeting
That I want to dance on mountain peaks
And shout Your praises!
I want to make a joyful noise,
Drumming every hollow thing I find
And chiming every round of metal or glass,
For all to come and see
For all to taste this glorious gift
For all to know this ephemeral, inexpressible
Quality of light; this blessing
From the Lord of the ineffable universe
From the one who is the Light of the world.

RECHARGED

Jumped in the car this morning, Lord,
Singing, joyfully ready to worship You.
But You know what happened next:
The disbelief, the jolt of panic,
The expletive I should have deleted
But spat out instead when the key,
Turned,
Yielded no response at all.
For a moment I was crushed
As if the car itself were on my back…
But You whispered to me, "Peace."

I was recharged

MUSTS

Some tasks are must-dos;
There are places we call must-sees;
We proclaim some things as must-haves;
And we know many aspiring wannabes.
Teachers list exam must-knows
Parents acquaint us with must-nots
Between our mights, maybes and shoulds
It's easy to feel tyrannized by others' gots.
Thank You, Lord, for cutting to the chase;
We have only one real must: to love, not waste.

GNATS

The sun is warming the air
The flowers are fragrant and lush
And everywhere I walk
I am besieged by clouds of gnats
Cyclones of midges,
And squadrons of kamikaze skeeters.
As I nurse the little welts they leave
And scratch the irritated nerves,
I think how You were assaulted,
Encircled, ambushed, plagued,
Beset by swarms of pestering folks
During Your days on earth;
And how You are still pelted, prodded
And stung
With complaints,
With insults,
With blame,
With questions,
With demands,
Enough to raise welts in anyone.
Yet You open Your arms to us all.
Always You say, "Come."

STILL LIFE

We decorate our walls with still life
We capture the moment with still shots
We stop the action with freeze frame
We halt bad attitude with a chill
And bad behavior with time out…
Because life is a river
Because moments are fleeting
Because action is motion
Because attitude is a powerful force
And because behavior is contagious…
We try to preserve the evanescent
And arrest the perilous.
Help us be good stewards, Lord,
With each breath You give.

THE RACE

Saturday the three-year-olds will run for the roses
Mint juleps will parch hot lips
Broad hats will top elaborate coiffures
Big money will change hands
And for a day hoi polloi will stand among gentry
To cheer the handsome runners to their goal.

There are many distractions along the rail:
Shouts, bright colors, billowing clothes, waving arms...
But running the race and finishing well
Are the tasks before us.
Keep us on track, Lord, so we can carry
Your colors to the winner's circle.

May 5

ONE VOICE

National Day of Prayer

I know You promised, Lord,
And gave us a rainbow as proof;
But I look around and wonder
Why You don't fold everything up
And just take it back.
Manufacturers run recalls
When things go awry.
The difference, of course,
Is that You didn't give us defects;
We drove ourselves off the High way,
Deeming our judgment better than Yours.
On this day I join my prayer
With many, many more,
And ask You, precious Lord,
To scorch all human hearts with repentance,
To clean out the God-shaped void
We have crammed with garbage,
To give us dreams at night
That will turn us from philanderers to prophets.
Recall the nations, Lord! Reclaim our hearts!

CONFIRMATION

I often wonder how we determine labels, Lord.
The proper way to name things of importance.
When our children proclaim their faith,
Name You as their savior,
Express their desire for church membership,
And seek to join us at Your table,
I wonder why we call this Confirmation.
Can we confirm what You alone can see, Lord?
Let us rather call it Affirmation,
For we affirm Christ's love and ours for this child.
And let us then call it Proclamation!
As we raise jubilant voices:
Hear ye, hear ye! We hereby proclaim:
Our beloved child stands before us all
To express faith in the inexpressible
To profess belief in the unbelievable
To embrace and be embraced by the body of God.
This is news to be trumpeted from city walls
To be posted on gates and pillars
To be carried home to every house
We have affirmed and proclaimed
Our family has grown today
And we are overwhelmed with joy.

UNSTOPPABLE

After March weather in May,
Today splendor has arrived
And beside all the Harleys
Roaring down the road,
Here come freshly waxed cars,
Their tops flipped back, rolled
Down or electronically stowed,
Their drivers exuberant,
Their passengers enthralled.
Convertibles, we call them.
Though I don't know why,
For no true conversion takes
    place.
Perhaps they should be
    transformables,
After those kids' robot toys…
Our French friends call them
Décapotables: de-toppables,
Which seems more accurate
(Though *capot* also means hood
And we wouldn't want them
Zipping around with engines
    exposed!)—
We might follow suit and
    call them
De-toppables, but when I smell
The fresh breeze, the new leaves
Of spring, the flowers along
    the way,
The glorious world You have
    given us,
Lord, I think untoppables would
    be best,
Because it also means we
    recognize
That wanting to be closer to
    nature,
Top down, is wanting to be closer
    to You,
Mighty Sovereign God, hat
    in hand
To feel Your fingers tousle
    our hair
And bless our brow with drops
    of sun.

FULL MOON

Some months, I admit, my focus slips
And I get caught up in my own railing
Against lunacy...
This morning's gauntlet notwithstanding
I remind myself to look up
And admire the luminous beauty
Of our mottled opalescent satellite
Our evening guardian and sometime day companion
Whose changeable state exhibits such constancy
Whose massive nearness compels the tides on earth
And we are drawn
Seasonally or daily
In phase or out
To reflect on the hands, the heart, the mind,
The love that gave us such a metronome.

BUSY

It's too easy to be busy;
To use up the hours in going and doing.
Help us, Lord, to breathe.
To breathe.
To breathe
Long,
Slow,
Steady,
Deep
Draws
That bring fragrant tastes of Your garden
That unbusy a frenetic soul
That calm chaotic impulses
That settle a churning heart
That gentle a rapid pulse
That reveal time unfurled, unmeasured, always open to You.

THEY SAY…

We hear it all the time, Lord.
Scientists and other pundits
Speak with authority,
Make pronouncements,
Publish test results,
"Prove" their cases…
Too often with assumptions,
Selected data, suitably weighted or curved:
Often with prejudice, in its truest sense.
Global warming, global cooling;
Limited resources, endless supply;
Eggs are good, eggs are bad, eggs are good…;
Animals have no language (can You imagine!);
Wars are necessary to win peace;
God doesn't have time to mess with the small stuff…
As if the choreographer of quarks and leptons,
The architect of galaxies and black holes.
The sculptor-poet-composer, the Mother of life,
Abandoned the baby at birth and walked away.
We really do like to hear ourselves talk, don't we?
Thank You for choosing to smile
At our childish solemnity about ephemera
And our churlish flippancy about immortality
And divine love.

BEARINGS

This morning, as I looked up from the kitchen sink
And saw that glorious creature lumber into the yard
I was exhilarated, Lord: a bear coming to call on me!
And wasn't I thrilled to find myself nearly face to face
As she approached the window, sniffing the air!
I wondered for a moment if she had brought peanuts
For the homo sapiens displayed in its natural habitat…
When she turned to forage through the backyard
Then I worried in earnest why, so early in the spring,
The bears are already scavenging the neighborhood
Away from the protection of their wooded home.
And I realized yet again, Lord, how we have erred.
You gave us oversight over Your creation,
Which we have burned, turned, razed and rebuilt.
And since we have dispossessed Your other creatures,
They have no choice, I guess, but to move in with us.

ANTICIPATION

It's one of our greatest pleasures
It's one of our greatest aches
So we say, "I can't stand it!" or "I can't wait!"
But we mean, "So exciting, isn't this great?!"
We talk about pins and needles
We watch the calendar or the clock
We tell You our dreams, our hopes, our plans
We ask You to bless our undertakings
And to grant our heart's desire
Yet to make our will the same as Yours.
Today two families prepare to join as one
It is a miracle only You could engineer.
Thank You, Lord, for the unexpected joys
Of intersecting paths,
Interwoven lives,
Entwined arms,
A new embrace.

JOINED

Today three precious couples
Are exchanging vows before You, Lord,
And the witnesses who love them, too.
Some of us will speak readings.
Some of us will sing.
Many will weep little tears of joy.
Most will marvel at how two independent adult lives
Can be joined, united, welded, wed
So easily, as gracefully as two hands clasp…
Then I remember Rodin's bronze *Cathedral*, Lord,
Those elegant, steepled hands pointing to You,
And I give You all glory, laud and honor
For it is You who make the two one.
Bless these couples, I pray,
With ever-growing love,
Never-ending tenderness,
Always-sharing respect,
Many years of good health
And daily bursts of laughter.

MOM'S DAY

Tall and small
Round and flat
Boisterous and placid
Hearty and frail
Ruddy and pale
Today we remember especially to say
We love our mothers
And we thank You, God,
For putting us in their hands,
In their arms, in their hearts.
It may be by birth,
It may be by choice,
But we are forever theirs,
Beloved, cherished, prized.
It saddens me, Lord, that for a few
"Mother" conjures bitter pain,
The anguish of rejection or abuse,
But we thank You, Lord, for the women
You provided instead, to befriend,
To soothe, to provide the missing care,
That no one may stay orphaned by love.
Today more than ever we treasure
The women who gave us life
One way or another;
Let us heap affection back upon them
Our mothers
Our mentors
Our models of love.

RELAY

It's graduation season, Lord,
The time when all-nighters,
Highlighters and palm pilots,
Yards of crumpled paper,
Reams of coffee cake
Are kneaded together
And rolled out...
Pressed into evenings of laughter
Pealing forth like cathedral bells
Epiphanies
Hallelujahs
The finish line where the baton,
A roll of parchment, is passed
And the runner carries on...

EXAMS

Doctors perform them
Forensics require them
Cheats sell them
Students sweat them
Proctors attend them
Professors weigh them
Mechanics computerize them
Officials undergo them
Witnesses swear to them
Juries scrutinize them
Decisions, decisions, decisions…
We learn to choose wisely
If not knowledgeably.

DRY

We've been hovering for days at the edge of rain
The forests are crisp and panting
Our towns are tinderboxes
And we barely dare breathe for fear of a spark
The pewter sky hangs so low
Its muttering spatters our windshields
I wonder how many beg You for water
To put things back in balance,
And how many still toss burning butts
As they speed blindly past.
Shower us, dear Lord; pelt us with rain;
Drown us with conviction, and save us
From our own malice and disregard.

TREASURE

Meditation
Deep reflection
Research and rumination
Consultation of scripture
Discussion with You, Holy Spirit
Deliberation
Consultation with tradition…
Mining for treasure
Then drawing the map
To put others on the same page.
Theology is a weighty task;
Serious business, some say.
But I thank You, Lord,
For such outrageous fun!

HELLO?

An unanswered phone is
Annoying.
Insistent.
Redundant.
Provocative.
Intrusive.
Shrill.
A little scary.
Compelling.
But I don't have to tell You, Lord.
You call us every moment
Of every day;
Yet we answer
So seldom
Or hang up
Too soon.

BEGINNINGS

It's nearly mid-year by our calendar
Yet we're in a season of beginnings:
Vegetable gardens
Cornfields
Prom romances
Summer novels
Construction projects
Vacations
Weddings
Commencements
And I am reminded
That the successful conclusion
Of each new start
Begins and ends with You.

HAVEN

Forgive me, Lord.
I forget too often to thank You
For Your endless gifts.
I am reminded today
To thank You for the comfort
The safety
The certitude
In spite of long distance
And the span of days
As I arrive at tonight's haven
And melt into the oh-too-seldom
But always so welcome embrace
Of brother, sister and niece.

May 22

SACRIFICE

We think we are civilized
Genteel
We faint at the sight of blood
So the notion
Of blood sacrifice
For the atonement of sin
Is as barbaric as burning virgins
Alive
To idle idols
We don't understand
How
A slow agony
On an instrument of torture
Worse than the rack
Can set us right
Back on track
With the holiest holy
The Ancient of Days
We don't think we want
A god who is appeased
By such cruelty
Yet every day
We get down off that high horse
To drool at carnage
On our many screens
Palm-held, desktop, laptop,
　　tabletop or wall-mounted
We buy games for our children
That teach them barbarity is
　　survival
We brake on the super-highway
To gawk at twisted metal and
　　broken flesh
Secretly hoping to see blood.

We can never rid ourselves
Of the bloodlust
The desire to see someone else
Bleed so we can escape
　　unharmed
We are more closely tied
To our less *civilized* ancestors
Than we care to admit
And we really do understand
The mystery of sacrifice

ANTS

We deprecatingly call them vermin
But we have much to learn from tiny ants.
They work in teams or alone
But we know when one appears
Many more are somewhere nearby.
A scout determines the work
And the prize,
Sends out the word,
And the relay teams report for duty.
There never seems to be backbiting;
We don't see sluggards or slackers
Or counter-productive detractors.
They know
Many legs
Make short work!

DANCE

It's remarkable, Lord.
We are all framed the same way,
With the same muscles and tendons,
The same neurons and dendrites,
Yet we move so differently!
Lithe or gawky,
Fluid or maladroit,
We dance before our God.
With the elegance of herons,
The powerful grace of horses,
The suppleness of panthers—
Or the tottering of penguins,
We dance before our God.
Solemn as sea turtles,
Playful as otters,
Plaintively, pleadingly,
Joyfully, awkwardly,
We dance before our God.
You set our straights and bends.
You formed us thick and thin.
You made the cool and the heat;
You gave us a pulse, a breath, a beat:
The rhythm of life.
You surrounded us with music and motion;
You even choreographed the stars!
We praise You,
We worship You,
We dance before our God.

PHOTOGRAPHS

Smiles or frowns
Giggles, dimples or scowls
Our families and friends
Are captured moment by moment
Then, with great pride,
These trophies, these prizes
Are mounted, to be hung on the wall,
Displayed on mantel or shelf,
Or squirreled away in books
Closed to the passage of time.
It would be easy to think, Lord,
That You put us in some album,
Archive us away for years
Without another thought
Until it's time to dust…
But You are nothing like us, Lord;
You don't need photos to treasure memories
Because You are simultaneously
In our past, present and future.
You are with us
Every breath, every day.
Every step,
Every stumble,
Every smile,
Every tear
Is etched on Your heart.

MOVING

It's scary and joyous
Laborious and energizing
Enervating and rejuvenating
Daunting and haunting
To pour over years of accumulation
Gifts and trophies
Purchases and handicraft
Prizes, surprises, even some booby prizes
We discover our roots are not permanent
But like mangroves
We are travelers in space and time
Our roots lie truly interwoven
In our history with You, Lord,
Not with family who can sever
Or friends who can betray
But with You first,
You last,
You foremost:
Our home
Our hearth
Our nurture
Our past
Our now
Our forever

MOVING DAY

It's hard to supervise, Lord,
To watch others labor in my place,
So I find myself falling into teacher mode
To anticipate questions with thoughtful, thorough instruction
To oversee the project without getting underfoot
To encourage, yet maintain the authority to correct
To be watchful without seeming distrustful
To appreciate with social appropriateness
So no one is befuddled
And no work is scuttled
And everyone is pleased with the result.

MOVING ON

Lord, You were there
You held my hand
You caught my tears
You hugged me close
Even when I pushed You away
My scarlet face twisted
Contorted
Ashamed of my pain
Lord, You were there
You held my hand
You caught my tears
As I locked the door
Where Daddy died
And said, "Goodbye, House"
For the last time.

May 29

VIRGINIA

Elon College to Chevy Chase,
As I thread the mountain roads
The air is heavy
Pregnant
Rain-fresh
Saturated with scents
Honeysuckle
Hot sausage
Wildflowers
Wet hay
Vineyards
New-mown grass...
I am surprised to find
Shade tastes sweeter,
Though moist as loam
And spiked with the cool iron smack
Of clay, peat and wet rock,
While sun patches
Are fragrant as steaming corn
Hot oil-slick asphalt
And horse leathers.
Thank You, Lord,
For this taste of unexpected delights.

SAFE

After a long journey
The way home always seems shorter
The heart quickens
Even an unmown lawn looks inviting
The household cries *Welcome!*
(Though maybe it's just the hungry cats)
And the bed fits so well.
I do wonder, Lord,
How this particular arrival—
With its many trips
To unload the cargo,
Beloved memories—
Could cause me
To leave the door
Wide open
All night…
Perhaps I wanted to share my joy
With the world;
Perhaps it was just a slip
Because I felt at ease,
So safe,
Still wrapped in family love
And sheltered in You, Lord,
My true home.

HOLIDAY

Thank You, Lord God,
For this day
This holiday
This holy day
This day of few obligations
And all choices.
Thank You, Master Planner,
For this day
This free time
This me time
This time unstructured
Unseamed
Unstitched
Loose and flapping in the wind
Of Your Spirit.

RELATIVITY

Ten days away from routine order
Seems like a month or more
So much has been packed
Into my travel bags and camera
How can it that no one else has stories
Out of the ordinary
And *nothing* has changed!?
Astonishing, I say.
How can this be?
Then I think about relativity
And how our eons are but a blink
To You, Lord,
Yet You lavish Your complete attention
Your eternal self
Your perfect heart
On every second of every human life.
It may be physics or metaphysics.
It may be philosophy or theology.
But above all it is a mystery
That I cherish.

HAND TO HAND

Any day
Every day
I know there are many,
Many people
Who need.
And hurt.
And cry.
Or hold back behind taut lips
Screwed down eyelids
Closed fists.
But this day
I ask You to extend Your hands,
To hold,
To heal,
To comfort,
To encourage,
To strengthen,
And to tickle with joy
The people dearest to me,
Who are tense before unknowns,
Feeling lost or angry or resigned,
Scared
As they pass through doctors' hands.
Is it selfish, Lord,
To put my own
Ahead of the world's forgotten
And abused?
So be it.
Today I am selfish
And ask
For abundant blessings
On those I love
Second only to You.

ON TRUST

Like faith
Like love
It's innate but quickly lost
In the crushing disappointments
And cruel betrayals
Of life.
Like faith
Like love
Recovering
Rebuilding
Relearning
Trust
Is a long
Slow
Tedious
Painstaking
Process
Of re-establishing
Relationships
Commitments
Comfort levels
And most of all
Proof:
Longstanding
Reliable
Wear-resistant
Time-triumphant
Ever-increasing
Evidence
Of trustworthiness.
Thank You, Lord,
For making us resilient
And hopeful.
And thank You, Lord,
For being our model
Of faithfulness
Reliability and
Constancy.

June 4

AN F-ING TIME

Full moon and a catastrophic accident
Five lanes of supersonic traffic
Frozen
For hours
Furious
Frustrated
Fuming
Fender bending
Finger pointing
Forsaking all laws and human kindness
Filching an inch here or a
Foot there, shooting
Filthy looks
Forgetting all civility
Furtively running shoulders and access lanes
Fueling vindictive payback.
Forget peace among men!
Forgive them, Lord,
For they know full well what they do.

June 5

MEMORIES FOR SALE

The day was beautiful, Lord.
Serene, sun-blessed, fresh with breezes
After a cleansing rain.
It was lovely
Touring unknown local neighborhoods
With my dear friend
Discovering tidy homes
Immaculate lawns
Gardens rich in colors and shapes
Stone-bordered ponds
Complete with waterfall or fountain
And the occasional frog.
It was fun to glance
At the bargain tables
And ground displays
Glimpse into someone else's life
The faded joys and the regrets
Offered, with hope, to new homes.

But what a change of mood, Lord,
When back home the tape told
Frightening news:
While we were at play
Our friend had been stricken with pain and fear
And while we were laughing,
Confiding,
Enjoying each other's company,
She was alone
In the ER
Waiting
Hurting
Waiting
And I wished she could have put that anguish
On a table
In a driveway
Boldly marked:
"Free or best offer."

PENTECOST

If it weren't for Your Spirit, Lord God,
There would be no indwelling.
There would be no inspiration.
There would be no insight,
For we are blind without Your light.
Ancient of Days, without Your Spirit,
We would have no desire for justice,
No sense of order, no concept of law,
No way to distinguish right from wrong.
If Your Spirit were not present
Among us, around us and within us
Your church would be aimless,
Your name would be forgotten,
Your praises would remain unsung
For we would know nothing about You.
Thank You, Holy Spirit, for coming
To heal us, to unite us, to equip us.
Fall fresh upon Your church,
Call us to be bold for You
And lead us forward,
Banners aloft, like flames on the wind.

LITTLE SURPRISES

Ladybugs on the windowsill
A caterpillar creeping by
The distinctive call of cardinals
And their splash of fire in the greens
Someone's cat dancing with a leaf
Animated by the same breeze
That wafts biscuits and coffee
Down the lane...
Thank You, Lord,
For the little surprises
Of an ordinary day.

June 8

CLUTTER

You know me, Lord. I am naturally chaotic,
Though I prefer to say I am creative,
With a mind full of ideas and concepts.
I'm always juggling several projects at once;
Surely it is natural that some clutter falls out.
Piles of stuff don't look good, I know;
I want to sweep everything into place
If company comes by
But I forgot where I put the place.
"A clean desk is the sign of an empty mind"
Says the popular office plaque
And so I am happy to remind myself
I am not the sole perpetrator of clutter—
Even as I set new goals for reining in
And corralling some of those wayward nags.
I think this time I should brand 'em
And ask You to help the fences hold.

KNIVES

Life is filled with contrasts and opposites
Isn't it, Lord?
Today two people You and I love
Will go under the knife
To be healed. And
Nearly everyone You and I love
Will lift a knife today
To prepare and to consume
Life-sustaining food.
Yet other people You love
But I do not know
Will be confronted with knives
Intended for no good purpose today,
Wielded only to threaten,
Intimidate, inflict harm and hurt.
It must sadden You beyond expression
That we so often abuse
Our freedom to choose
To follow You:
The only way to make the cut.

SHARING

When we plug in a lamp and turn it on
The light can be seen from adjacent rooms,
Sometimes from other homes,
Occasionally from a distance.
The thing that strikes me, Lord,
Is that we never know who's looking
Or even who might need the comfort
Of that simple light.
I thank You, Lord, for the joyful
And humbling surprise tonight
When, though I prayed quite personally
For my friend at her hospital bed,
Her screened-off roommate
Gratefully said, "Thank you.
Your prayer was for me, too."

June 11

SCHOOL'S OUT

My schedule is a little less hectic;
My life is a little quieter;
I can sleep in on Saturday,
See friends almost any night of the week;
There are fewer books to scan
And gulp, highlighter in hand,
More books to savor and digest.
Daylight lasts longer—
The possibilities seem endless!
Lord, as much as I love school,
Thank You for this interlude,
For the discretion to use this time
For rest, relaxation and renewal
Before the autumn labors begin.

VERBOTEN

Brownies, ice cream, M&Ms
Strawberry cheesecake,
Brown sugar, banana bread.
Some pleasures are just forbidden.
We know it's for our own good
But certain days, Lord, it's just so hard
To toe the line.

THE WORD

Reading Your Word,
Dear Lord,
To the church
During worship
On a Sunday morning:
What an awesome joy!
For a few minutes I am Your voice.
Actor, storyteller, prophet,
Parent, teacher, priest…
The power of Your words
Rivets them,
Breathless,
Eyes wide,
Hands open to catch
Hearts ready to hold.

MONDAYS

Mondays are for beginnings
And continuing what carried over
Mondays are transitions
From sabbath to service
From worship to work
Which is just to say
Love with a shoulder to the wheel.

TUESDAYS

Tuesdays are for details
Ticking off Friday's last chapters
And getting focused
On what matters.
Tuesdays are settling time,
Hitting stride,
Moving ahead,
Breathing deeply, Lord,
Centered in the joy of doing
What You have gifted us to do.

WEDNESDAYS

Wednesdays are for perspective,
Looking back and peering ahead.
Wednesdays are for taking stock,
Balancing accomplishments against goals
And action against plans.
Wednesdays are for tweaking,
Tuning and decision-making.
Wednesdays are wandering in the wilderness
On the way to the promised land.

THURSDAYS

Thursdays are for reflection,
Testing the wind,
Tacking the sails,
Turning the rudder...
Or holding steady.
It all depends on You,
Because You are the Compass,
The Centerboard,
And the Wind.

FRIDAYS

Fridays are for departures,
Closing files,
Pink slips,
Retirement parties
Or vacation starts.
Friday is also for celebration:
Many call it pay day
And party night.
For others, tonight means Sabbath:
Candles, prayers and worship.
Fridays are week's end;
Eyes drowsing shut
As mouths yawn open...
Bless this Friday as You bless every day,
Lord, as a closed book on the past
And a fresh page,
Pen in hand.

SATURDAYS

Saturdays are for family
Hallowed days of play
Summer picnics and water splash
Fall leaf chasing and pumpkin patch
Winter snowballs and sleigh rides
Spring gardens and fragrant nights...
Saturdays are for catch-up
Brush-up
Pack-up
Stay-up
Hook-up
Above all look up...
To You, Lord of all our days,
Guardian of all our nights.

SUNDAYS

Sundays are for praise and renewal.
Sunday is the day of gathering:
When all the teams come together,
Raising many voices as one,
Huddling to hear the Coach's plan,
Pledging loyalty,
Chanting battle cries
And bursting out toward the field
In readiness to meet the foe.

ROADBLUR

Everyone's in a hurry.
We drink instant beverages;
For supper we nuke a chunk of ice;
We drive big wheels at huge speeds
As we zoom from task to task.
Overnight isn't fast enough,
So our mail is electronic.
Research is mouse-clicks away.
Cell phones are the universal NOW.
The air is saturated with chat:
Tasteless vulgarity shouts down
Courtesy and decorum.
Help us, Lord, to slow.
To take the time to know
Each other's heart.
To let Your grace flow
Over us, like a blanket
To tuck us in for a long sleep.

FRUSTRATION

It's not so much the technology
That baffles me, Lord;
It's the incapacity
The insufficiency
The inability
The insouciance
The insolence and apathy
Of those who are placed to help
But seem to be either illiterate
Or irredeemably, willfully ignorant.
I know I sound like a snob, Lord,
But is it too much to expect
People to do what they are paid to do?
Take my anger and make it love
Take my bitterness and make it sweet
Take my despair and give me hope
Take my critical eye and fill it with tears
Of sisterhood and compassion.
I have to call again tomorrow!

THESIS

The berber in my office is brown;
It has been brown for years:
Practical. Nondescript. Unassuming.
Boring.
But today, Lord, I saw.
The miracle is that You opened my eyes
And I saw
The millions
Alongside millions
Of beautiful threads:
Ebony, chocolate, chestnut, sienna,
Cream, cinnamon, coffee, rust,
Ginger, russet, cherry, burgundy.
I'm almost ashamed to tread
On these throngs of unique individuals
Woven together by the craftsman's hands.

ANTITHESIS

Soup and stew are many merged into one.
Many flavors, consistencies, colors,
Many textures and nutritional values,
Chopped together
Seasoned and flamed
Until they begin,
Like pet and owner,
Like husband and wife,
Like old friends,
To lose distinction,
To look alike, to blend, to blur,
Nearly fused in identity,
United in purpose.
Just as the unique members of Your Body
Are unified by the fire of Your Holy Spirit.

SYNTHESIS

The awesome thing, Lord,
Is the way You bring together
Scores of uniquely gifted
Yet uniquely challenged people,
Fill our voids with Your abundance,
Consume our dross in spectacular fire,
Place us in teams of headstrong and weak
And teach us to pull equally
In the same direction.
What could so easily be bedlam,
A souk of competing egos,
Under Your guidance
Becomes harmony in motion.

PRAYER

Squeaks and squeals
Sobs and sighs
Whispers or wails
Pleas or angry rant
Wordless tears, wringing hands
Lines etched in our memory
Or spontaneous outpouring from our heart
Secrets, shame, regrets
Joys, dreams, desires
Simple thanks
Overwhelming praise
Silence
Until You speak.
Peace.

REMOTE CONTROL

You know how we make jokes
About those pushbutton sticks,
The symbolic struggle for power,
For it is the one who has the remote,
The bearer of the scepter,
Who dictates the speed and direction
Of channel surfing,
Directs the volume or may even mute,
Imposes the program on all present,
The powerless, passive mob.
There are some who misunderstand
Our dependence on Your power, Lord,
As if Your rod and Your staff were clubs
To bludgeon us into submission!
There are so many renegade goats,
Too busy butting heads to realize their pain,
Too proud of their supposed freedom
To ask Your protection from the wolf.
Transform those goats into sheep, I pray,
And let them long to say
"Your rod and Your staff, they comfort me…"

COBBLESTONES

Some are round, some are square
Some rectangular, some hexagonal
Some have no particular shape at all
Worn smooth or broken
By centuries of feet
And a procession of wheels
How like Your children, Lord,
These billions of stones
Each uniquely beautiful
No matter how cracked or worn
Each more useful in the company of others
Than alone.

STEPPING STONES

Both decorative and practical
Stepping stones are flat
And fat enough
To hold the largest foot
Safe from errant ways.
Markers of the way to go
Memories of where we've been
A trace
A trail
A path
A guide
Footholds against danger…
Thank You, my Lord,
For walking the way first
That I may follow in Your steps
And thank You for leaving behind
Large, solid, inviting, secure
Stepping stones
To keep us from going astray.

PROCRASTINATION

"Later" seems to be an adult's favorite word
Days are crammed with tasks and voices
Clamoring for time and attention
Priorities rule
(Necessities first)
So promises often get shredded
By the tension between *should* and *can't*
Then thrown into a bag for mending.
Children and animals know only "Now".
Lord, forgive me my Laters
I pray, and use my Nows
In new ways
For Your glory.
Let Today always be Your day.

GIFTS

Present, prize, token of affection
Remembrance, celebration, memorial
Reward, souvenir, commemoration
Award, donation, assistance,
Contribution, ability, capacity
Skill, talent, faculty, bent
Facility, knack, genius...
We can develop it by doing
We can hone it at the whetstone
We can practice it to improve
But a gift by definition begins
With the Giver alone
And can be no other than what the Giver gave.
Thank You, dear Giver of gifts.
Help us to use every gift wisely
In love
Just as You intend.

TERRITORY

Lord, I'm reading about Jabez
And how he prayed so simply
So boldly
Asking just four things:
Your blessing
Your increase
Your hand upon him
Your protection.
And You said Yes.
Thank You, Lord, for the faith of Jabez
For the chronicler who recorded his prayer
For the patriarchs who made it canon
For the man who noticed it amid pages of *begots*
And the publisher who made public his book
For the singer who turned it into music
For the studio that recorded his song
For the radio station that put it in my ears.
Indeed You have answered Jabez' prayer
You blessed him in life and in death
You enlarged his territory into the 21st century
You put Your hand upon him
And protected him from the pain of oblivion.
I do not ask to be famous, Lord,
I do not wish to be a millionaire
But I pray that You will enlarge my territory
That I, too, may be a blessing to others
That they may know the comfort and the power,
The touch of Your hand.

BLACKOUT

Dangerous skies
Violent winds
Massive downpours
Sudden lightstrikes
And thunderquakes
Huge rumbles
Then calm
Bright blue
Birds back
Cool breeze
Gentle lull
Cats at the sill
Ceiling fan hums
Dryer drum tumbles
Any afternoon in summer
Till
Pop!
Silent
Power-less
Dark
Shrouds the house
Throwing me a century back
To candlelight
And reminding me
As I open Your book
There is only one endless power.

INDEPENDENCE

On this day of patriotic pride
We are bombarded by joy:
Star-spangled banners
Red, white and blue bunting
Parties, parades, picnics…
The culmination for most
Is fireworks against the night sky.
Yet we seem to have forgotten
That freedom means everyone's
Life, liberty and pursuit of happiness,
All of which require responsibility
And self-control for the greater good.
On this day of patriotic snide
To protect their independence
And their illegal fireworks
Two brothers used lead pipes
To crush the cranium
Of an off-duty peace officer
Who lived just down the same street.
Lord, bless the martyrs of true freedom,
Burn out evil from self-righteous hearts.

FIREWORKS

They're going off in my living room
As the cats and I jump with every boom
And fly from window to window
With each snap, crackle and pop.
The rockets' red glare
Is snaking over the deck
The bombs bursting in air
Shower our roofs with sparks
And wrap our many trees in smoke
And the repeated high-pitched whine
Has set the nearby dogs howling
I am trying to be patient
I am trying to appreciate their joy
But I can't celebrate
My joy is crippled
By my neighbors' selfish disregard
For their neighbors' safety and peace of mind

PASSIONATE

Lord, let me never be lukewarm
Or half-hearted
About the things that matter
Increase my ardor
Nurture my zeal
Let me be fervent,
Vehement when necessary,
Always vigorous in Your service.
Protect me from the contagion
Of indifference or apathy.
Keep me keen
Hone my passion
That it may always be for Your kingdom.

WARNING

I got a warning this morning
The state trooper stopped me for speeding
Well, no, actually. To be more precise
He said it was for not slowing down
After I had seen him.
And Lord I was thinking, How absurd!
The tailgaters and gatecrashers
Who buzz us, push us and hound us
Go free because they jump lanes
And stand on their brakes,
Pretending to be model citizens,
All the while putting the rest of us
In greater jeopardy than before,
And because I continue, honest in my sin,
I get stopped for refusing hypocrisy.
"I know it's hard to do the speed limit,"
He tells me, writing out a warning slip.
The rest of the journey, driving only five above
I had to flash hazard lights
To warn the swarms of speeders
To peel around as I crawled down the road,
Constantly in harm's way.
I'll be asking You all day, Lord,
What the warning was really about.

GARAGE SALING

A time of fellowship
Sisterhood above all
Out and about
Prowling the streets
Scouting yards and drives
For the unlikely pleasure
Of inspecting someone else's junk
And the occasional eureka:
A dollar scarf
A ten-cent brooch
A two-bit paperback
Our eagle-eyed friend
Navigates unknown neighborhoods
Engages strangers in warm conversation
And spreads joy wherever we go.
Thank You, Lord, for sunny Saturdays
And simple pleasures
For shoestring budgets.

SERVICE

Lord, thank You for all who come to Your house
All who come to worship You with gifts of praise
Thank You for those who serve with loving hearts
And for those who have learned to accept with grace.
Thank You for the outspoken and for the meek
For the whole and hearty as for those ailing and weak
Thank You for young and old, timid and bold
We have so much to share and to teach
Yet still have many things to learn from each
Thank You, Lord, for those who question with open minds
And for those whom You enable to respond in kind.

H_2O

A symbol of birth and rebirth
Cleansing, both outside and in
Contained in clouds, it shrouds us
Until it falls to nourish and refresh
The core component of our bodies
It also covers most of the earth
Placid and inviting
Or seething destroyer
Barrier or pathway, enemy or friend
It is both life and death
And then, oh Living Water,
It is life again.

MEASURING

(Luke 6:37-38)

Measuring stick
Measuring cup
Measuring out
Measuring up…
Why, I wonder
Are we so obsessed
With size? Acquisition,
The only gauge of success?
Why do we mark off,
Carve up and grab land,
As if we could truly own
The creation of Your hand?
Why do we compete?
Why do we compare?
We might as well bottle
And peddle the very air!
Your prophet Isaiah asked
Who has measured the waters
In the hollow of his hand,
Or with the breadth of his hand
Marked off the heavens?
Who has held the dust of the
   earth in a basket,
Or weighed the mountains
On the scales and the hills in a
   balance?
Oh, that Your majesty and mercy
Would be our focus instead!
Let us say, with the psalmist,
My mouth will tell of Your
   righteousness,
Of Your salvation all day long,
Though I know not its measure.

We are so very small
In the scope of Your universe
Yet You lavish on each of us
An eternity of love,
An ocean of grace.

HYDRANGEAS

They're everywhere this month,
Huge pompoms of round petals
Exploding out of dark green huddles
To cheer passersby.
Some are chalk white, like peppermint;
Some pink, from pale barely there bubble gum
To hot magenta, intense, alive, volcanic;
Others are blue, from nearly blanched summer sky
To brilliant sapphire, like Paul Newman's eyes.
Most are either or, but some bushes can't decide
And offer all. How can this be?
The color of their blooms, I've been told,
Depends on the pH of the soil, acid or base,
Or neutral in between.
How like us people, I think;
We range from conservative to liberal,
From optimist to cynic, from poet to pragmatic,
From faith-filled to "not for me".
With lots of fencesitting in between.
Turn our soil, Lord, and rain down what we need
To blossom into such beauty that all will stop
And ask the name of the gardener who grew such joy.

COFFEE

It comes in many flavors now
Some natural, some added;
Different strengths, roasts, grinds—
Sometimes I think it takes a graduate degree
To be able to choose. It's intimidating.
Like church for so many people,
Lord, and like Your written Word.
They walk near, attracted by the aroma,
But they are afraid to ask for a taste,
Too overwhelmed by choice.
Keep the pot on, Lord, to percolate
And help us to put some samples out
For weary souls who gravitate
To our café but are afraid to step in.

REVOLUTION

Today is Bastille Day
And my friends joyfully remember
The day their Revolution began
They cast off their shackles
They tore down royal idols
They marched on the great fortress
And freed the wretched prisoners
They began a great experiment
Claiming:
Liberty!
Equality!
Fraternity!
Yet even the noblest cause
Is eventually tainted
By greed, power, politics.
There will always be masters
And servants:
Liberty is a relative term;
There will always be hierarchy:
Equality has its limits;
And there will always be Others:
Fraternity is a family thing…
Until every soul knows You,
And learns that only Your love
Is the true equalizer
And the true revolution.

CABARET

It's marvelous theatre
Beautiful music
Sweet, sad, satirical, stirring
The most lyrical song
Raises hackles as it is repeated
Clever staging
Entertaining dance
We laugh, we clap
Like the cabaret audience onstage
And perhaps envy a little
The free lifestyle and bold style
Of these 1930 Berliners
This show is far darker than it first appears
The danger is insidious,
Creeping in from within and without
Like the evil at the core of the story
Our story
Human history
I noticed many people ran away
At intermission
Like the people onstage
They didn't want to face the truth.
No mystery there, Lord.
We prefer candy coating and ribbons
To swastikas, death camps
And the cross.

BLIND SPOTS

We all have them,
Don't we ever!
So we get blind-sided
By both good and bad
As we cruise our own road
Thinking ourselves safe,
Under our own steam,
Our hands on the wheel…
Today I preached about
Mule-headed, blind Bible men
And how You made them see.
My Lord, today and every day,
Keep me from giving in
To the tunnel vision
Of my stubborn self
And help me to look
Through Your eyes
Farther. Wider.
Open my eyes
To each dark corner
Of my own self
And let me welcome
Your light
Even there.

FAMILY

They say blood is thicker than water;
But life has taught me
The heart knows family
Not by bloodlines or DNA
But by love freely given
The way people choose to cherish
The way strangers, some foreigners,
Can be caught up in open arms
Embraced
Enlaced
Intertwined
Grafted in to the family tree.
Thank You, Lord, for my ever-growing list:
Blood relatives, yes, but also
The kith and kin of faith, heart and soul.

SCABS

They're ugly and obvious;
We want to hide them,
But they need to be aired.
Children pull them off
And often eat them
To destroy the evidence.
We say we hate imperfection,
Blemishes are repugnant;
But scabs are God's canopy
Over the construction site
Where healing takes place.
It's a slow process, repair,
One we impede every time
We remove the armor
Of temporary skin.
Creatures of habit,
We pick at or try to conceal
All our blemishes,
Especially the kind called sin;
Even though we learn as kids
That scratching and peeling
Not only delays healing
But also creates scars.
God is ready and waiting
To mend our wounds, sores,
Imperfections and willful scars;
But we have to allow people to see
The signs of God at work.

PAINT

What a remarkable thing is paint!
Depending on the shade,
It may quietly envelop us,
Creating a peaceful environment
For relaxing and letting go…
Or it may be loud, calling attention
From far away, beckoning some
Yet sending others on the run…
It covers everything it touches
Changing outward appearance
Slightly or immeasurably,
According to the need.
It protects what it covers
From outside influence,
From rot and decay.
God's hand on our lives
Is a little like paint;
But what He pours out on us
Penetrates deeply, is absorbed,
To create inward transformation
When we accept His touch.

CRIME

Another friend has been burgled, Lord.
She is devastated
They dared to enter the intimacy of her home
While she was sleeping!
They took nearly everything she owned
Even her purse and all it contained
They took her identity, Lord,
And drove themselves away
In her car!
And You know better than I do
How she feels
They might as well have beaten her
Because she couldn't feel more abased
Or wounded
And, Lord, I feel incapable
Insufficient
Unable to help her see You are there
Unable to convince her
To drop into Your waiting hands
I pray that You will,
As always,
Do what I cannot

TRANSLATION

Translation seems to be the theme du jour
Language to language
Culture to culture, or counter
One perspective to another
Concept to concept
Metaphor to concrete
Or vice versa
Sometimes the borders are transparent
And we can peek across
But usually the barrier is solid
Rendered impenetrable by habit
By stubborn resistance,
Whether arrogant or ignorant.
Translation is midwifery,
Opening the way to transformation
Facilitating metamorphosis
But You are the light of meaning
And the only Agent of change.

July 22

HONOR

Oh, Lord, my Lord, I know You are worthy of all honor and praise!
But today I began to wonder just what *honor* means.
You are the great Physicist, Engineer, Inventor,
Worthy of every person's *respect*.
Artist of infinite creativity, You have our *awe*
And our abject *admiration*.
In this fallen world, imagine: we *credit* science
As if it were a sentient being
Capable of organized thought and accomplishment!
Your *reputation* is perfect, although some people
Give You bad press for not pulling our strings…
But it is Your love for us, Your parental courage
And devotion, that leaves us free to make choices
Especially the wrong ones
So we will learn to turn back to You with *reverence*,
To pay You *tribute* and express our *esteem*.
I *venerate* You, Lord God,
I *revere* You,
I *hold You in the highest regard* possible to this mortal mind
And so I honor You with praise and devotion.
Hallelujah!

GLORY

It's a word we use fairly often, *glory*.
We call our flag "Old Glory",
We sing "Glory, Hallelujah",
We mutter "glory, glory"
(Lest a "Lord, Lord" be taken for a swear)
We talk about glorious weather,
Or flowers, or victories…
But I wonder if we really know
How beyond human scale
How immeasurable, unspeakable
Superbly unplumbed and infinite
Is Your grandeur
Your magnificence
Your majesty
Your wonder
Your glory
Dear Lord!

WORSHIP

How hard it must be, Abba God,
To see Your children prostrate before idols.
We value commodities and achievements
We esteem power and title
We revere craftsmanship for its value in trade
And we crave the vestments of prestige
We venerate stars for their glamour and wealth
We create our own little gods
That, like golem, grow into hungry giants,
Consuming every resource we have.
Call us swiftly, Lord,
Summon us with power
That we may bring the sacrifice of praise
Pour out our first fruits
And express our love for You and You alone.

SEWING

A needle can pierce a thread
And may carry it awhile
Before sliding through,
Leaving the thread behind,
Broken or frayed,
Less itself than it was,
And unable to do its job,
Which is to strengthen and unite.
A thread must have a needle
Whose eye will frame it
As the needle carries it
Exactly where it must go.
When the thread is sewn
It gathers and confers
Strength beyond its own.
Lord, always be my needle
And keep me in Your eye
That I may do as You intend
In the fabric of earthly life.

BRUISED

I have always bruised easily
An occasional prod in the arm,
A firm hand on the shoulder,
A close encounter with a doorjamb…
Capillary fragility, they call it.
I call it black and blue.
Yellow, green and purple.
Marks of life lived
Passing evidence of encounters
With anyone or anything
Entering my personal space.
I have always bruised easily,
Soft, like a banana or peach,
Simply crushed or damaged,
Especially under the skin.
When I want to toughen my hide,
Lord, keep me soft and pliant,
Let me yield when necessary
And forgive
Always forgive
Those who bruise
Intentionally or not.

LATENT STORM

The heavens are filled:
Everywhere I look,
Layer upon layer
They hang
They hover
Ready to release
Any time now.
Dark, swollen, brooding
Like knitted brows,
The thunderheads gather
And wait
Charged
To drop their burden
Of bolts and rain
Riding, driving
Down the rivers of wind…
I am awed, Almighty.
I am awed.

TEETH

I have a mountain in my mouth today
Where a broken half slope had been for weeks
I feel as though that once broken tooth
Is now twice as menacing in its post-avalanche
Crowned form. More a miter than a crown.
But teeth of another sort are gnashing
And snapping today in my town.
Local power jocks, political self-promoters
And abusers of grace are poised
To dig metal bucket teeth into sacred ground.
In the name of progress and child welfare
They want to destroy 12,000 years
Of ancient American history
It would be a travesty, Lord,
If it weren't so tragic, so cruel.
We respond with what teeth we have,
With words, spoken and written.
And words lifted to You.
Because their teeth are bare gums to You.

PRIORITIES

Lord, I wonder what it must be like
To have all eternity to devote to each person,
Beast, bird, each blade of grass.
Your attention is lavished, moment by moment,
Equally, on everyone and everything.
Your love is poured out in blessings.
Parent *par excellence*, You nudge
And guide, correct and protect,
All the while giving our freedom total respect.
I look at the projects I must juggle,
The commitments and promises I've made,
And the things I would like to do
If there were more time...
I see how easy it is to shift priorities
(No harm intended, of course)
Or to simply forget what I said
And meant to do.
Lord, protect me from wanting to please
And set me instead on living to serve.
I know then my priorities will be clear.

MOONS

Although no longer a distant mystery,
It still mesmerizes us
As it comes and goes,
Grows and fades;
This faithful nighttime companion
Sometimes shows its beaming face
In broad daylight,
As though oblivious
To the natural order of things.
And it makes me think
About satellites
And orbits
Mass and gravity and tides…
How we all orbit others whom we admire,
Thinking ourselves gadflies merely;
Yet we, too, affect them
With our presence or absence
Our support or opposition.
Without each other for balance,
Without the Master's hand,
All orbits would decay.

CONDITIONS

We condition the air
We condition our hair
We condition our pets
We condition our bets
We condition our children
We condition contracts with if/then
We condition our bodies
We try to condition our minds
We bargain and barter; we tease
Evil, always expecting You to bind
Satan from grabbing our souls.
Self-deception is a deadly game,
Especially when we choose to forget
You wrote the conditions centuries ago.

TIME

We surround ourselves with timepieces
That mete out the minutes and hours,
The soldiers in our platoon of days.
We put them on our walls and desks,
Our mantels, cars and bank towers.
We wear them on our wrists, our waists,
Or hang them from our necks.
We chime the hours by carillon
And have institutes to chart any variation
In the clockwork of the universe
That gives us our sense of years…
Instead of glorying in the poetry,
The mobility of Your creation,
We imprison ourselves in rigid regulation;
We idealize the beat of a different drummer
As we march stolidly along,
Wishing away what time we have.
Kindle in us a sense of eternity, Lord;
Ignite our souls to take flight beyond the bars…

August 2

NETWORKING

We do what we can for others
What You equip us to
What You call us to
But sometimes we need to
Do nothing but listen
And sometimes we need to
Pass the baton
To one who knows what we do not
To one who can what we cannot.
In the press and stress of life,
Dear Lord, remind me every day
That I am only one limb in Your body,
One digit or one organ,
Able to do only what You purposed for me.
Remind me always:
Apart from fellow members,
And apart from You,
We all die
Useless.

NEWS

Journalists have choices every day.
It is tragic that the business of selling news
Has shaped their decisions
And given the public less value,
Less information for life,
Less essential reporting,
Less professional integrity,
Less prophetic proclamation.
Lord Jesus, God's Word incarnate,
Help us redefine our desires
And curb our taste for Schadenfreude;
Help us reclaim and reform the machine
That spews out the words and pictures
We expect to be truth.

August 4

THE WEB

"Web" used to be a simple word
To represent something woven
Something strong
Something useful, resilient, stretchable
Yet which always returns to its natural shape.
Spiders spin them for lair, nursery, and snare;
Weavers loom them for cloth or belting
For fashion, furniture or industrial installations;
But now the Web is a network
For research and education,
For access to anything the human mind
Can conceive and desire
For the display of all that is good
And evil
In the human spirit.
Lord, You gave us great minds
And pioneering hearts,
You have allowed remarkable technologies
That shrink the world.
Teach us now, I pray,
To teach each other
That since we wielded the first rock,
Every tool people have made
Has two potentials.
Help us, mighty Shepherd,
To prefer building and sharing
To destruction and conquest.

RED

Red is the color of exuberance
Joyful celebration
Birthday balloons
Kites over the golden beach
Sweet summer fruit
Red is the color of passion
And fire
Flushed faces
Also the color of shame.
Red is the color of STOP!
Warnings, alarms, pain...
Red is the color of blood, spilt,
But also lobsters, cooked,
The timeless pleasures
Of sun-rich tomatoes and wine.
Red is the color of vehicular speed
And power
It is also military might
Or political leanings.
Red is the color of Pentecost,
Episcopal church doors and
Your Holy Spirit present within us.
Thank You, Lord,
For the vibrant, febrile, delicious,
Dangerous color red.

BARRIERS

"Good fences make good neighbors,"
We like to quote Mr. Frost as we dig holes
And plant posts, whistling into the wind.
But the fences we build
Are usually not for common good.
They are immutable factors
Of discrimination at its worst:
Class, color, style of speech,
Income, acquisition, style of dress,
Politics, theology, style of life,
Labels, tags, epithets...
Anything to differentiate
Anything to self-elevate
Anything but a handshake.
Lord, help us to break walls
To gate fences
To reach across borders
To mingle and merge
So we can emerge
Stronger together
Than apart.

TAXIS

Taxis are transport for hire,
By the minute or by the mile.
For a fee, they move us
From departure to destination.
Taxis is a different kind of movement,
A compelling attraction
Or a repelling aversion.
Different origins,
The first is *tax*, from the Latin for *touch*;
The second straight from the Greek
Meaning *to arrange*.
And I'm thinking, Lord,
What a wonderful arrangement
You have made,
Compelling us to help carry others
From a bad place to better,
And nurturing in us a repulsion
For wrong stops along the way.

FLAME

The attraction and the terror are inevitable:
Even the smallest flame has huge power.
It is light,
It is warmth,
It can release pleasant aromas,
It is beautiful in its dance with lady air;
But like some creatures,
It also destroys its partner
As it licks up her oxygen
And spits out what is left.
It is vibrant in hot colors,
Yet its heart is cold blue.
When we ask You, Lord,
To set our hearts aflame,
Keep us, I pray, from straying
Too near the cool of calculation
Or too far from our purest fuel,
Which is You.
Let us always be Your light
In the world,
Igniting new candles
To worship Your Name.

STATIC

"Love never fails..." she sings
As I speed the highway to work
But over and under her sweet voice
And gentle string background
Comes blaring hot rock
With its blatantly carnal words
And super-amplified noise.
"We cry, 'Holy!!!
Worthy is the Lamb!'"
I hear through a brief window
In the ceaseless assault,
A glorious tenor voice:
"We cry, 'Holy!!!
Praise to the King!'"
It's not just a battle
Of powerful transmitters
And overlapping frequencies;
Increase Your troops, Lord,
And keep us armed
For this ever-present
Always escalating
War.

NOT

It is my observation, Lord,
That we have established
At least two generations of people
More than oblivious to prohibitions;
To them the negative command
Is a complete fiction.
All things are allowed;
Anyone who disagrees is brain-dead,
A moron or a reactionary freak.
I used to think public displays
Of Your primary commandments
Are outlawed because reading them
Convicts the guilty conscience.
I realize now it is simpler than that:
They are meaningless; they contain
A word that has ceased to exist.

Maranatha! Come soon, Lord!
Rescue us from "permissiveness"
Before we plunge into the abyss.

SPOILER

"Spare the rod, spoil the child." Samuel Butler,
based on Proverbs 13:24.

Look at Your babies, Lord.
We drive our own buggies now.
Mix our own formula
And declare ourselves diaper-free.
Just yesterday an infant,
Rattle in hand and blabbering away,
Careened past in his black pram—
Nearly nondescript, really,
Except for its huge pushhandle
Looming over the back!
And, Lord, how I wanted to see
Your hand reach down from heaven
To grab that handle,
Lift that carriage, wheels spinning,
Seize that talking, button-decked rattle,
And give that rambunctious boy a paddle
Because no one else will.

CHANGE

Alice said, as I recall,
"I knew who I was when I got up
But I seemed to have changed
Several times since then."
Spare me, Lord, from any day
So dull, so safe, so tedious
That I did not grow or diminish,
Blush or blanch,
Cross swords, then
Wave the olive branch...
Engrave or efface,
Assert or withdraw,
Mourn or rejoice.

SNEEZE

As normal as hiccups and gas
(Those horrid explosions of inappropriate,
Uncouth and unwanted noise)
We casually toss a thoughtless blessing
At the one whose face is red,
Heart is pounding
And hand holds a hankie
Sodden with things we prefer not to name.
It's a curious mechanism
You've given us, Lord,
That periodically turns the imperturbable
Into a magma-spewing volcano.
Even a dainty "achoo" is an interruption
In the natural flow of life,
A pause,
Like punctuation,
Full stop.
Look around.
Intruder alert.
Damage control.
How excellent are Your ways, Lord!

BROADCASTING

We think nothing of it
We are surrounded by messages
Borne on and retrieved from the air
Radio waves
Satellite dishes
Telephone cells
Video towers
Live feed
Everyday words
Routine occurrences
It has become ordinary experience
To transmit and receive
Data and images through space and time;
We even know about radio emissions
Across the universe
And the light of distant stars
Reaching us eons later...
So why, I wonder,
Is it such a stretch
To accept that God
The Creator of space, time and talk,
Can send and receive messages
Invisibly and at will?

APPLES

Lord, thank You for the apple trees,
Centuries old, frail and gnarled,
But faithful bloomers and givers of fruit.
Thank You for the orchard keeper
Who first planted them so long ago
And thank You for the builder
Who respected them as he erected my home.
Thank You for the arrhythmic pelting rain
Of hard green marbles, hailstones,
Yellow-green golf balls,
And the breathtaking silent beauty
Of the does and fawns
Who decorate my lawn at night
And the heart-skipping wonder
Of the black bear mamas and cubs
Who come to dine
When they think
No one is looking.
Thank You, Lord,
For letting me see,
And for letting them stay
Calm and curious
As I speak words of welcome
And love.

THE CAFÉ POETS

The poets fly into the room
And mill about
Like birds on a wire
Chittering, chirping, preening,
Exclaiming the news,
Jumping back and forth,
Electricity in the air:
Tonight they will speak
What they have fashioned
With everyday tools.
Tonight they will preach
To the choir;
And hallelujah, Lord!
We who teach Your truth
Want to hear what others proclaim;
We who sing Your praises
Need their voices to stay on key.

WIRES

The computer lab is a nest of snakes,
Coiled or slack,
Slithering out of wall outlets
Slipping into surge-suppressing power strips
Striking up into ports where they sink their fangs:
Plugheads and pinheads.
Many colors, sizes and shapes,
They undulate and slink along walls
And floors, and linger across desktops,
Or hang about in mid-air...
I think about all the power
The data, the dreams.
The images and information
The messages of hope and love
The decisions that affect billions
The multinational strategies
The keystrokes of war and peace,
And I wonder, once more,
At the ways evil can sabotage innocence,
And I marvel at the assurance
That Your love has already won...
Which is why snakes are cursed
To creep along, on their bellies, in the dust.

SAVED

Like terror
Like hope
Its persistence was admirable,
Unstoppable—
But for brief pauses to rest
And renew, to continue assault.
The butterfly, naturally black
  and blue,
Pounded every inch of
  transom glass
Looking for a way through
To the beckoning blue sky
All the while, poor creature,
Oblivious to the great doorway
Thrust open
Mere inches below.
My new friend knows the answer,
Offering a leafy green fern
Picked from the front porch,
As she stands
Precariously perched
On a stepstool
Borrowed from the closet
And she proffers the fern
Above her head
Hoisted to the heights
Of this stately hall
Until the valiant warrior
Settles
So gently
So softly
So slowly
On a frond.
We are then able
To carry it to freedom
From the glass prison
Where glimpses of heaven
Had beckoned and enticed,
Frustrating our flighted friend.
Liberty was unattainable
Without intervention:
The grace of a loving gesture,
The patience to wait
For it to come,
To light,
To trust,
To rest in our hands, so to speak.
Its surrender led to freedom,
My friend and I its door to salvation
From false promises.
Stopping to think like a butterfly,
To meet it in the air with a gift of life,
My friend was anointed to reach
That lost, laboring, fragile being,
Just as You, Lord, became human
So we might see You clearly
And turn from our fruitless strife
Into Your arms, waiting to
  transport us
To the heaven we seek.

SINGLE

On the days I feel sad to be single
I remember that I am not alone
And I praise You, Lord,
For being my Helpmate,
My Protector,
My Defender,
My Advisor,
My Guide;
And I thank You
For holding my hand,
For smoothing the wrinkles of my life,
For soothing my fevers with a cool breeze,
For reminding me:
You have surrounded me with love.
Family, friends, a caring community of faith.
But most of all
You pour Yourself out to me daily,
From the cross to the cup
You envelop me in a bridal veil
And call me Beloved
As You break the glass under Your heel.

COMMITMENT

Promises are broken every day
One's word is, alas, of little value
When handshakes are made with fingers crossed
Deals are made for double-cross
Contracts can fall through loopholes
And attorneys squirm into wormholes
To rewrite history...
We teach our children to lie artfully
We entertain ourselves with clever coups
We are proud to pull off a scheme
Or to cheat a cheater at his own game
Commitment is only until you get what you want.
We like to believe we deserve better
So by hook or by crook we'll get there.
Alas, Lord, we pretend so well we forget
What we deserve is exactly what we'll get.

ABOUT TEETH

Gears need 'em
Dogs bare 'em
Politicians lie through 'em
Hens don't have 'em
Grins show 'em
Taffy slows 'em
Cops & ME's study 'em
Gift-getters shouldn't check 'em
Punches loosen 'em
Nutshells break 'em
Your Word has 'em:
Strong enough to bite
Through the toughest skin,
Grind down the defenses,
And shine out
Like the pearly gates.

P'S & Q'S

I just learned the origin of
"Mind Your P's & Q's"—
English pubs, it seems.
So I thought, "Of course!
Pence and quid..."
But I was leaping away
From the obvious
Pints and Quarts.
The tally has to be right
At the end of the day,
Dispensed vs. taken in
And I thought again
How fortunate we are
That through faith in Jesus
We don't have to sweat out
The P's & Q's of Your talley sheet;
We have a clean page
Every day
In Your ledger book.

CHAIRS

Like people,
Chairs come in limitless variety.
Sizes: height, width, depth, footprint...
Colors, shades, textures almost beyond naming.
Shapes: square, round, oblong, delta;
Curved, straight, angular, bent.
Spare, hard, a no-nonsense tool
Purposely utilitarian;
Or plumped, cushy, soft, inviting:
A friend for long hours of study or story.
Some are pliant, quietly folding out of the way;
Some scream to be the focus of all.
Like people,
Chairs come in limitless variety,
All designed and crafted to serve,
To support,
To hold,
Each in its unique way.
How sad, Lord, are the empty chairs,
Arms extended,
Waiting to do what they are meant to do.

TIMEKEEPING

Calendars and clocks
Seem to rule our lives
We mete out our attention
To projects and people,
Set obligations to timers
That tick tick tick until ding
We're "done"
Ready or not
Time to move on.
Relentless demands
Inflexible schedules
Agendas, planners, palm pilots
Even our secretaries need clerks
To police appointments 24/7…
I want to scream out
"Get me a stopwatch, Lord!!!"
Not to time efficiencies
Or start another race. No.
Let's literally stop the watches,
Stop the meters,
Stop the clocks,
And take all the time we need
To realize
It was You, Lord God,
Who created all timekeepers,
To remember it was You
Who drew their orbits and
Set them all in motion;
To ponder
That You once stopped the sun,
Midday, mid-sky, mid-war,

For about a day
Because
Only
You
Are
God.

MAKING MUSIC

Even if we don't whistle or hum,
We make music wherever we are.
Patting or pounding,
Knocking or slapping
Hollow things and solids...
We are surrounded by drums
That beg to thump against our hands.
Life throbs with irresistible rhythms
That we pick up with our own
Tapping feet and snapping fingers.
Typing hands click across a keyboard;
Cloth rustles cloth with every move;
Even our pockets chime in with
Jingling change and jangling keys.
Instead of oppressing,
The percussion of life
Fills us with childlike joy.
Thank You, Lord, for poetic sounds:
Crumpling paper, sliding drawers,
Squeaky chairs, slamming doors;
A wet finger run around the rim
That makes a crystal glass sing.

WINGS

When I was quite young
I flew up to heaven every night
Then down toward a new earth
Where I was always welcomed
By my other family and friends.
No visible wings
Yet I could soar with great ease
And enormous joy.
The last visit
I remember so distinctly
Was bittersweet.
They filled my hands with gifts
And sent me off with many hugs;
The first seconds of waking
Were exhilarating as I remembered
With anticipation…
Until I looked down
At my empty hands
And wailed my unrecoverable loss
To the deaf walls of my room.
My wings were snipped
And the souvenirs were stripped away
I think now as I look back
That I needed to be sentenced
To walk the earth
So my soul would crave its memory
And seek to soar.

COBWEBS

Our classmate challenged us
To "find God in the cobwebs"
And I found myself caught
Suspended
In a fragile construction
Of image and word
As I focused my mind's eye
On those mysterious
Delicate
Intricate
Prolific
Seemingly random
Geometric arrangements of dust.
The complexity of the web
That seems to be woven
By an unseen artisan
With no apparent tools
Is just one of the tiny miracles
That escape notice
And, once seen, get wiped away.
But when the light hits the web
And the dust sparkles like diamonds
I catch a glimpse of heaven.

ON DUST

Our classmate challenged us
To "find God in the dust on the sills"
And I found myself reassured.
With an inclination toward entropy
And laissez-faire in housework,
Dust kittens are my frequent companions.
My schedule is filled to the brim
With projects more immediate,
While the grey silt accumulates in corners,
Rests on shelves, marches across the mantel,
Accusing me of sloth…
But today, looking for You in the dirt,
That fine powder settling out of the air,
Leads me to think of the remarkable cycle
You set in motion on Creation day:
"Of dust you were made, to dust you shall return"
Because our earthly bodies are ephemeral,
Merely tents for our nomadic souls
Which ultimately find their home in You.

August 29

DEAD LIGHTBULBS

Our classmate challenged us
To "find God in a dead lightbulb"
And I found myself perplexed.
What does God have to do
With a fragile bubble of glass
Greyed from within, burnt
By that final burst of light
And now, with its broken filament
Tinkling idly against its thin walls,
Useless for anything but the groom's foot
At a Jewish wedding?
Intrigued and persistent,
I thought some more,
And what pleasure there is, Lord,
In the moment of connection!
I am the dead lightbulb;
Even when I am fresh from the package,
Clear, bright, ready to shine,
Without You, I shed no light.
And when I am broken inside,
Burnt out, clouded over,
Frangible and brittle,
Only You can restore me
And set me as a beacon
To draw others to You.

YESTERDAY

Those who do not study history,
The proverb says, are doomed to repeat it;
So I look back each day,
At my life and Yours,
To learn what I can.
Help me see with Your eyes
That I may admit my wrongs
And set them right;
That I may recognize Your hand
In the good I thought I did;
That I may perceive the rudder
And the compass You put in my life;
That I may know You each day more,
For nothing about You is trivial, Lord.

TODAY

Today is the day that has never been
And will never be again
Today is the day of choices
And the beginning of their effects
Today is a day of consequences
From yesterday's yes, no and maybe
Today is Yours:
Use me as You will.

TOMORROW

Aside from the occasional prophet
(Who is, after all, Your mouthpiece
To the estranged world),
Only You know what lies ahead.
It is a fool's errand:
Such a waste of today!
A display of narcissism
And a total lack of faith
To worry about tomorrow
For You have already told us
Who of You by worrying can add a single hour to his life?
And again *Therefore do not worry about tomorrow,*
For tomorrow will worry about itself.
Each day has enough trouble of its own.
I am quite content, Ancient of Days,
To leave all my tomorrows to You.

September 2

A GATHERING PRAYER

Ancient of Days, we gather to praise You.
We gather to worship You.
We gather to love You.
We gather to learn from You.
We gather to serve You.
We gather to hear Your voice.
We gather to share Your presence.
We gather to celebrate Your sovereignty and Your grace.
Accept our praise.
Accept our worship.
Accept our love, as You first loved us.
Accept our ignorance,
Accept our prejudices,
Accept our stubborn willfulness,
As we put them at Your feet;
Teach us Your ways.
Bless our service,
That through us You alone will be glorified.

September 3

MEDITATION ON PSALM 27

The world will always beat us up.
Even our closest friends and family
Will, at some time, insult us,
Embarrass us, try to imprison us,
Attack us or walk out on us...
You are our only constant.
You are our High Tower, our
    Fortress.
You are the source of our hope,
Our joy. Our peace and our
    security.
The world will always tempt us,
Tell us lies, try to seduce us away
    from reality
Into a utopian fantasy.
Our money, our attention,
Our affection are all commodities
That the world wants to
    bargain for.
Our only true knowledge
Of who we really are right now,
And who we were called and
    equipped to be,
Comes from You, our Alpha and
    Omega.
We live in a world where
    everything is NOW:
Instant oatmeal, instant coffee,
Instant communications,
    immediate response,
Immediate retaliation, instant
    judgment;
We have forgotten the
    importance of planning.
We have forgotten the
    importance of preparation.
We have forgotten the
    importance of waiting.
We have forgotten the
    importance of patience.
The good news is that You, the
    God of all creation,
Want to be on intimate terms
    with each of us.
The good news is that You will
    always be there for us.
The good news is that waiting for
    You is not dead time,
It's growth time!
Wait for the LORD, my soul; be
    strong, and take heart,
And wait for the LORD!

PAUSE

Sometimes we say most in silence.
Poets and musicians know
Often the true message hangs
Between the lines.
In the rests.
In the emptying and filling
Of the breaths.
In a world where void is a terror
Noise is de rigueur and images shotgun
More rapidly than we can process,
Quiet
Must give us
Pause.
Rest.
Sanctuary.
Solace.
Insight.
It is in the hush
The stillness
The wait
That we hear You
Most distinctly.
Quiet me, Lord.
Call me into the deep stillness
Of Your arms
And sing me Your lullaby
Your love.

TASTE

We taste and see that You are good!
And although You are never-changing,
Our appreciation grows more refined,
More sensitive,
As we crave the elemental,
Essential and esoteric flavors of You!
We delight in the aroma of Your presence.
We savor the sweet,
The salt,
Even the sour tang
Of Your Word.
One day,
Quite unexpectedly,
We realize the bitter is gone.

September 6

SIGNS

The sign at the edge of my garden,
Under the mailbox,
Beside the road,
Proclaims scripture for all to see.
It was provided, joyfully, for free;
The verses change periodically,
Most often by unseen hands,
As the sign attendant comes and goes
Faithfully making his rounds,
My sign just one of many under his care.
The self-proclaimed pagan
Who lives next door
Views the sign with hostility,
Deeming it a personal offense.
This week, it seems,
She is furious. "Did you see?"
She asked a mutual friend,
"What she's saying to ME???"
I smiled at the report
And thanked You, Holy Spirit,
For giving me this sign
That You're chiseling away
At her stubborn heart of stone.
I went back to look;
Toward her house it reads:
"The fool says in his heart
There is no God."
Hammer away, my Lord!

September 7

BEST

Snapple is "made from the best stuff on earth."
Best Foods would seem to claim no one is better.
We are always pledging to do our best
Sometimes our *level* best, we specify.
Dogs have best in class and best in show.
Phi Beta Kappa keys reward best students.
We have best friends
Though they don't always survive
The challenges of time;
Even movies have a Best Boy.
This little word that we bandy about
Is the superlative of "good"
And if no one is good but God,
How can anyone or anything be more
Or most
That which is solely characteristic
Of God?

FOOD

At the diner,
Cars come and go in an intricate ballet
Like bees at the hive
They negotiate the intricate maze,
The ins and outs of the parking space.
Like planes taxiing to take off
And circling to land
It is constant motion yet orchestrated
As if led by an unseen hand.
Ironically
A mere hour before
I had seen concertgoers arriving
At a quite large church
Unable to accommodate the sea of cars;
A barrier dammed the lot
So the overflow was pushed off,
Backing up the tributaries,
Or shunted toward other sites.
The hopeful had to swim against the tide
To stand five-deep in an endless line.
So it seemed to me,
As I waited at the diner for my friends to arrive,
That the food more precious was far harder to attain...

September 9

DETAILS

"God is in the details" it is said.
I never understood that as a kid
And didn't get much more insight
As the years sped by.
Most people mean it as a reprimand
Or a rule of thumb for self-discipline.
But today it begins to make sense
As I consider: You made the cardinal
That sits chirping in my garden
In his brilliant red robe and black cravat;
You made the seeds that bring him there.
You provide the sunlight and the rain
That nourish the trees and bushes
To shelter this bird and his mate.
You gave me the ability to hear
His arrival, the vision to see his beauty,
And the mind and heart to appreciate
My winged neighbors, the shape of leaves,
The smell of fresh apple juice,
The gentle caress of the breeze,
All the tiny details of Your love.

CLOSE

Most of us like to be cuddled:
Hugs are reassuring, energizing;
A pat on the arm, shoulder or back
Is encouraging, a gesture of praise,
A touch of acceptance and love.
We allow the people we trust
To come close, crossing within
Our invisible walls of protection.
We say that we want to be
"Nearer my God to Thee"
But we really want You at bay
Yet at our beck and call
As if You were our pet or appliance.
Forgive us, Lord God. You know
Why we keep our distance.
Your presence is an all-consuming fire
And an all-revealing light.
We cannot stand Your scrutiny
Yet we so desire Your love.
We want to know You, but skitter
At the first signs of Your approach.
Intimacy is hard to achieve among mortals:
As ardently as we wish it, we wonder
If we can ever be completely at home
With the boundless God who came
To earth in the most unassuming way.
How foolish we are, precious Lord!
How close to us You want to be!

UNFORGIVING

A meditation on Job 1-14

"Curse God and die!" she says to her spouse
With rancor and malice
No doubt thinking about all her own losses
By association; how far the mighty had fallen.
I can hear her spit her disgust through curled lips,
"Feh!" as if her heroic husband were vermin.
And his friends are no better!
After displaying true brotherhood
By sitting with this pariah in the ashheap,
Making themselves as unclean as he,
One by one they turn on him,
Judge him for what has befallen,
And give him such detestable counsel,
God might have considered giving them over
To Satan's trials, were God as unforgiving as man.

SHOCK

The acts are unspeakable
The loss immeasurable
The pain immutable
The reason irrational
Here
Thirty miles from the crater
That was, only hours ago,
The twin colossi of the New World,
We walk aimlessly
We talk incessantly
We look with wide eyes
As we hang on every radio report
And try in vain to make sense
Of the senseless.
We take what comfort we can
By sharing our woe.
We see too clearly,
In the careful planning
Of this devastation,
The appalling brutality
Of human hatred
Unleashed.
Help us gentle our hurts,
Help us heal our ire,
Help us forgive,
Dear Lord,
That we may
One day
Learn to join hands
And live.

September 13

AFTERMATH

Aftermath, aftershock, post-traumatic stress…
We have many terms to describe the reality,
No, the surreal, unfathomable, oppressive pain
That looms over us like a pall,
A death shroud pulled tight as a lid.
A few enraged and misguided souls
Have engaged in the Roman tactic of decimation,
Although it feels more like the slightly more ancient
Greek annihilation—the attempt to destroy utterly,
To reduce to nothingness, to cancel, to void.
But like the periodic attempts to destroy God's people,
A remnant remains.
Evil may congratulate itself,
But
Though we walk through the valley
Of the shadow of death,
We will fear no evil
For You are with us;
Your rod and Your staff, dear Shepherd,
They comfort us.
You prepare a table before us
In the presence of our enemies.
Your anoint our heads with oil;
Our cup of blessing overflows.
Surely goodness and love will follow us
All the days of our lives
And we will dwell
In the house of the LORD
Forever.

COMMUNION

Praise to You, El Shaddai,
El Elyon, Almighty Most High,
You protect and preserve us
In spite of ourselves
You call us as servant-leaders
To catch tears,
To embrace firebrands,
To speak words many
Would rather not hear
And which we sometimes
Would rather not say;
You bless us with gifts
That wear so well they increase
    with use;
You fill us with love
So dynamic, so power-full,
That it erupts and pours out
To blanket all who pass nearby...
Praise to You, El Shaddai,
El Elyon, Almighty Most High,
For the communion of fellow
    believers
For the overwhelming comfort
Of corporate prayer
Especially when human history
Writes its darkest chapters
And we are asked to explain.
Praise to You, El Shaddai,
El Elyon, Almighty Most High,
For the bread and wine we share,
The exquisite communion of
    intimacy,
Even though, I admit,
For a moment or two
The elements lay heavy on my
    tongue;
My throat, saturated with
    sobbing tears,
Refused further passage
And I remembered that bleak
    moment
When You asked, "Let this
    cup pass
From me..." then willingly went
    to the cross.

MAYHEM

I remember a folktale told in my youth,
How a traveler lost in the woods
Is hosted by a forest elf
Who brings him in from the snows
And marvels as the man warms
His hands with hot breath,
But then cools a bowl of boiling soup
By blowing across it—
The elf is terror-stricken,
Wondering what manner of beast
This is who can blow hot and cold
With the same breath…
Surely we must be frightened
By our own ambivalence;
We reach out hands of peace
And succor, yet we steal from victims,
Gather evidence of the anguish
To sell by the chunk…
Human evil is held in balance
By human love
But the scales tip every day
The other way.
Help us, Bread of Life,
To come to Your table together
To negotiate no more;
To accept instead the only peace
That conquers evil,
Transforms fear into love
And opens the gate to eternal joy.

September 16

CLOSER

"*We just don't talk anymore,*" You say.
"Nothing to talk about," I retort.
"*You don't have time for me,*" You say.
"Can't You see I'm busy?" I snort.
"*Don't you love me?*" You ask.
"You know I do," I grumble.
"*You take me for granted,*" You say.
"Not at all," I protest weakly.
"*You ignore me until you need something.*"
"That's not fair," I snap, although I know it's true.
"*You don't really know me,*" You say.
"I'll never understand You," I snarl.
"*It takes time and commitment,*" You caution.
"Just what I need," I mutter, "More commitments!"
"*Only the one you've already sworn,*" You say.
"Are You saying I've let You down?" I pout.
"*Is that what you think?*" You say quietly.
"Well, I have missed some dates with You."
"*While I waited patiently,*" You add.
"I'm sorry. I didn't mean any harm," I say.
"*It hurts our relationship when you forget me.*"
"Is it too late to make amends?" I ask, a little shaken.
"*Not at all, my child,*" You say. "*Come into my arms.*"

WOE

I noticed long ago, Lord,
With the new eyes You gave.
It happens every year!
Good Friday
And Yom Kippur
The most solemn days
In the life of Your people
The holiest days of Your covenant
Relationship with us,
Year after year,
The heavens brood
With somber clouds
That frown and drag,
Sag across the skies,
Heavy with the impending
Sorrow of human sin.
Yom Kippur, the day
We atone for twelve months
Of defiance, with prayer,
Fasting and pledges to obey.
And Good Friday, the day
You atoned for all time,
For all people, as You
Shrugged off Your divinity
To shrug on our iniquity.
The load was heavy against the nails,
And so all nature bleeds with You,
And weeps its mighty woe.

September 18

CLOSER STILL

"Oh, for a closer walk with Thee" we chant,
But the syllables no longer seem to mean
Anything but notes we have sung for years.
You are always present
You are always near
Your Spirit is as close as our breath
Your Word, which reveals You to us
In remarkably nuanced ways,
Is always as close as our night table,
Our desk, our lap, our memory...
And You are always waiting to hear us speak,
Keen on our desire to hear You respond
Yet we are so lazy, Lord, even afraid,
Like the naughty children we are,
Unwilling to hear Daddy chide.
Like spouses who have drifted apart
We fear the hurt of cleaning our festering wounds.
We forget the joy of knowing You
The peace of Your hand upon us
The comfort when You hoist us to Your shoulders
To walk awhile, away from the dangers
That draw us far from You...

September 19

GETTING TO KNOW YOU

While we are mortal, we are limited.
We are stitched to the edges of time.
Our knowledge, like any database,
May be nearly infinite in potential
(You've given us curiosity and dreams!)
But it is utterly finite in capacity.
Our vision depends on where we stand.
Every generation learns anew;
It's not a refusal to learn from history,
Rather a need to learn to walk
Each person for herself
From crawling to tottering
To running, with all the falls between.
Our limitations bind us to earth and each other
But also stimulate our hunger to get beyond.
In this life, You know we are incapable
Of absorbing and comprehending
The limitless, infinite, eternal nature
Of Your glory, Your grace, Your love.
How wise You are, merciful Lord,
To give us only a little of Yourself at a time
The way You showed Your back to Moses
As You passed by his shielded eyes.

AN UNGATHERING PRAYER

Bless Your servants, as we go Your way,
Keep our eyes on You, lest we stray.
Use our hands and words as Yours;
Prepare the path, and open doors.
Engrave Your Word in our hearts.
Protect us from Satan's poison darts.
Grant us joy when we feel strained;
Grant us peace in times of pain.
Make us a blessing to someone today,
God, Christ, Spirit, these things we pray.

FIAT

Horses power
Flowers bloom
Trucks transport
Thunder booms
Waters flow
Bells ring
Lamps light
Choirs sing
PCs display
Kids pout
Dogs behave
Cats go in and out
Weeds grow
Birds fly
Flies buzz
Pans fry
We worship
We praise
We serve
We raise
Our voices
With one accord
To tell the world
Jesus is Lord!

PARADISE

Lord, we know, though seldom admit,
That we not made for mortal life.
We have the imprint of eternity
In our genes.
A racial memory, perhaps,
Of the days when You walked with us
In the cool of the evening
Among the trees You created
For our shade, our shelter,
Our sustenance, our play.
How I long to walk with You,
To hang on Your words as lovers do,
To gaze at Your face
And find the smile reserved just for me.

September 23

AUTUMN THOUGHTS

As I look at the exquisite beauty
Of our late September landscapes,
The crisp colors of the dying leaves
Like licks of flame fanned by the wind
That rips them free from the branches,
I wonder why.
In spring, when all is born anew,
You give us gentle greens:
Sage, celery, olive, lime, jade…
Relaxing, refreshing, soothing hues.
In autumn, nature's death dance
Is a spectacular frenzy of hot dabs:
Red, scarlet, crimson, chestnut, claret,
Orange, pumpkin, ginger, carrot,
Yellow, lemon, gold…
I used to think it was a bonfire
To warm our thoughts in advance
Of winter's bleak cold.
Today it dawns on me: You speak
To us in nature. Fall's show
Is the vibrant end of Your rainbow,
The profile of Your light.
Death is coming, You remind us;
Choose now: the eternal spring of faith in Christ,
Or the endless, winter burn of a godless place.

CIRCUMSPECT

Retreat means
Withdraw
Pull back
Run away
Give ground
Recoil
Leave
Vacate
Abandon...
Sometimes we need
To recede, to recoup, to recover;
Sometimes we need
To drop everything and give way.
When we retreat to meditate,
To learn from one another,
To learn more from You,
We pause to breathe,
To refresh our spirits,
To seek more intimacy
With You, dear Shepherd.
When we retreat to give up,
We leave behind the gimmes,
The wannas, the haftas,
The shouldas...
And we give in
Completely
Ceding all control
To You, our Commander in Chief.

LIONS & LAMBS

Lord, we're in such a hurry
We're impatient with the lessons of life
We're tired of trudging uphill
Especially when we stumble and roll back
You told us there would be wars
And rumors of wars
If we were less egocentric or ostrich-like
We would have noticed long ago
The world is an eternal battlefield.
Some of us have convinced ourselves
We're in Eden restored
As though our exile weren't permanent
And the gates of the garden sealed from sight.
But since the machines of war
Have come to our shores
And left bloody tracks across our land
We are crying out in one voice for that day
When the lion will lie down with the lamb.

POETRY

My Confessor,
My Forgiver,
My Comforter,
My Guide.
My Teacher,
My Way,
My Truth,
My Life.
My Light.
My Light!
You have gifted me with poetry—
Such an awesome responsibility,
Such a thrilling joy.
A pale reflection of Your creativity.
You spoke everything into existence;
You challenge me to speak the intangible onto paper.
Like You at the genesis of all,
Words are my tools *and* my material—
Like my ancestors, I dress stone with stone.
Prayer is the ultimate poetry,
The expression of the inexpressible,
The telling of the unfinished story.

September 27

TALK

Waking, washing,
Eating, driving,
Working, watching...
I am always talking to You,
In my heart of hearts,
And I am always listening for Your voice.
You know there are times
When I feel distant, drifting, drowning...
The times I have walked away from You,
throwing my hands up in frustration.
The times I have sought You unrepentantly.
The times I have accused You of being unfair,
Or forgetting someone I love,
Or throwing me to ill winds.
The times I have simply ignored You,
Choosing to be my headstrong, rebellious self...
Yet, gracious God, I still know
With unshakable certainty
With immutable tenacity
With absolute temerity
That You will never abandon me.
You will never turn a deaf ear to my voice,
Whether it be praise, worship and thanksgiving—
Because You deserve no less
And far more than I manage to offer—
Or intercession, because there are always
So many petitions I feel compelled to bring You;
Or simply the chatter of a good chum
Enjoying the fellowship of her most constant Friend.

FALLOUT

In their anguish and terror,
Many people blame You for recent evil;
It breaks my heart, dear Savior,
That they fall prey to further evil—
Believing the hypocrites
Who say such acts are Your judgment
On our country, the new Sodom—
They fall prey to further evil
Instead of turning to You for solace.
And wisdom.
And longer vision.
But already I see some positive fallout:
In spite of the horror, because of the horror,
More people are willing to hold the hands
They used to spit on—to get help,
Or, more's the beauty, to offer it.
More people are inclined to invoke Your name
With awe and homage
Who used to casually toss it around
Or spew it on others as invective.
More people pray, even publicly;
More people run to You, Daddy God,
Looking for salvation from this moment.
Grant them, I ask,
A hungrier heart
To learn about the salvation that matters
For eternity.

POST-TRAUMA

It is always the surprises of life
That set us looking for deeper meaning
That remind us You are the author of our lives
That ignite our passion
To know our individual role in human history.

INSIGHT

Since I have been writing psalms,
I have learned to see You in the tiniest glimpses
And in the broadest vistas.
In the moist corner of an eye
And in the warmth of hail-fellow-well-met embraces.
Through my morning aches and evening yawns.
In the comfort of Your presence
And the challenge of interfacing with those
Who would challenge Your *curriculum vitae*.
Continue, I pray, to make me a blessing.
And do keep me from being a burden.
Let me only be an obstacle
To those who need to trip over faith
In order to look up to You.

October 1

ASSIGNMENT, PART 1

A prayer in the wake of September 11, 2001

Kind. Omnipotent. Just. Mother. On September 12,
These are the words I selected from an assigned list
Of attributes we commonly ascribe to You, God.
We had to choose the 4 least appropriate to describe You.
It was a very difficult choice to make, Almighty.
You are the source of all my joy, all my hope,
All my strength, all my comfort, all my vision, all my wisdom,
All my sense of what is right, what is important, what is lasting, what
    is fleeting…
And because all the terms offered to us are appropriate and true,
How could I choose 4 to say I am "least comfortable" with them?

In that week of unspeakable, unthinkable malevolence,
In that week of anguish and sorrow,
In that week of human tragedy and inhumanity,
It seemed appropriate to say I am not so comfortable
With the description of You as *kind*.

Not that I blame You in any way for what human hands had done;
That would be as cowardly as the perpetrators of that evil.
No, it is because *kind* is such a wimpy, insufficient term,
In the context of Your limitless reach, Your constancy,
Your selfless love, Your infinite mercy
On us narcissistic, rebellious children.
You rain down blessings on us every day,
Yet we shake our fists at You
Or turn our backs and pretend You are not.
You had Your Son pack away His glory for a time,
To be born into our tiny world,
To walk among us,
To heal bodies and hearts,
And to go willingly to the scorn and agony of the cross,
Weighed down with our unrighteousness…
Calling You *kind* just is not ample enough
To express the scope of Your grace.

October 2

ASSIGNMENT, PART 2

A prayer in the wake of September 11, 2001

In that week of terror and human weakness,
It seemed appropriate to say I am not so comfortable
With the description of You as *omnipotent*,
Compared to omniscient, omnipresent and omnisufficient.
It is not because I doubt Your power, dear God;
No one and nothing in all Your creation rivals
The dynamic creative power
Or the potential destructive power at Your command.
It is merely because the other descriptions are so much more apt
To express the qualities we rely on and cherish in our God.
You know everything about us—our comings in and our goings out,
The number of hairs on our heads,
Our every need, our unspoken thoughts.
In Your unbounded love, You watch over us;
You hedge us into the sheepfold;
You protect us (as far as we are willing to accept) from the wolf;
And when we insist on straying, You seek us,
Give us tender care and healing,
And offer to bring us back to the fold.
You are everywhere at once,
Because You are the Master of time, not its servant.
You are always accessible, ever with us,
To the end of time and beyond.
And You are all-sufficient, the answer to every question,
The period at the end of every sentence.
You are Light, Love, Breath.
You made us, You sustain us, and You rescue us from every snare.
You lift us from mourning to joy.

ASSIGNMENT, PART 3

A prayer in the wake of September 11, 2001

In that week of vengeance and human injustice,
It seemed appropriate to say I am not so comfortable
With the description of You as *just*
Because the justice we arrogant children deserve
Is too great a punishment to think about;
I look instead to Your mercy and grace,
Your love and forgiveness.
Our Lord and Savior Jesus took the rap for us;
He did the time so we can walk free.
Too many people that week,
And still now,
Are crying out for justice, meaning vengeance
And retaliation.
An eye for an eye, a tooth for a tooth…
Almighty Creator, thank You for setting aside judgment
And giving us a Lifeline direct to You.

ASSIGNMENT, PART 4

A prayer in the wake of September 11, 2001

In that week of impotence and dependency,
It seemed appropriate to say I am not so comfortable
With the description of You as *Mother*
Only because it is alien to the culture in which I was raised,
Where You are always addressed as *Father*.
Jesus always called You *Father*.
As much as I cling to Your maternal nurturing,
It is very difficult, I must admit, to call You Mother.
You know my heart;
You <u>know</u> it's not a matter of gender, God,
Certainly not one of hierarchy.
It is merely a convention of language and concept
That has become very difficult to break,
As it would be if tomorrow my nation ruled
That henceforth *blue* shall be called <u>red</u> and *red* <u>blue</u>.
Would it diminish or augment my appreciation
Of intense, vibrant primary color? Not at all.
It would merely confuse my ability to name.
You have so many other names--
My Defender, my Shield, my High Tower--
Surely it does no harm,
Dear Parent in heaven,
That I like most to call You Abba, Daddy.

ASSIGNMENT, PART 5

A prayer in the wake of September 11, 2001

In that week of reflection,
Reaching out and reaching in,
It seemed appropriate to say
The only restrictions
On my description of You
Are the limitations of human language
Which must by definition attempt
To delineate the immeasurable,
To label the ineffable
And to characterize the unfathomable.
Thank You, Eternal One,
For dipping into human history
In Word, in Person and in Spirit,
So that we may know You intimately
In spite of our own limitations.

October 6

BREATH

My Confessor, my Forgiver, my Comforter,
My Teacher, my Guide, my Way,
My Truth, my Life, my Light!
You have gifted me with poetry—
It's an awesome responsibility
And a thrilling joy;
I liken it to a pale reflection
Of Your creativity, Lord.
You spoke everything into existence!
My challenge is to speak
The intangible onto paper.
Words are my tools *and* my material—
As though, like pre-industrial beings,
I dress stone with stone.
And prayer is the ultimate poetry,
The expression of the inexpressible,
The telling of the unfinished story.
You are my source *and* my destination.
You are the path I walk.
You are the Word *and* the Poem.
You are my breath.

TRANSFUSION

You are the health of my heart,
Oh, Lord my God!
My surgeon and my healer!
You carefully remove
All that is dead,
The clots, the plaque…
And You drain out my blood,
Which is infected with sin,
Transfusing it with Christ's blood,
Holy and clean.

SABBATH

Gracious and merciful Lord,
You have commanded us concerning the Sabbath day,
To keep it holy.
Loving Father, You are concerned for us, Your hyperactive children.
You know better than we do
How important it is to routinely
Stop
And
Rest.
Rest.
Rest.
Some of the best music happens
In the rests.
I am humbled before You,
Creator, Composer, Conductor of Life:
As I lie down to rest in Your wings,
I lift my song of praise.

CHATTER

Waking, washing,
Eating, driving,
Working, watching…
I am always talking to You
In my heart of hearts,
And I am always listening for
    Your voice.
You know there are times
When I feel distant,
Drifting,
Drowning…
The times I have walked away
    from You,
Throwing up my hands in
    frustration.
The times I have sought You
Unrepentantly.
The times I have accused You
Of being unfair,
Or forgetting someone I love,
Or throwing me to ill winds.
The times I have simply
    ignored You,
Choosing to be my headstrong,
    rebellious self.
Yet, gracious God, I still know
With unshakable certainty
That You will never abandon me.
You will never turn a deaf ear to
    my voice,
Whether it be carrying praise,
    worship and thanks—
Because You deserve no less
And far more than I manage to
    offer—
Or imploring pleas of
    intercession,
Because there are always so
    many petitions
I feel compelled to bring You;
Or simply the chatter of one
Enjoying the fellowship of her
    most loving,
Most faithful,
Most forgiving Friend.

EXPLETIVE DELETED?

In their anguish and terror,
Many people are blaming You for recent evils;
It breaks my heart, dear Savior,
That they fall prey to further evil
(By believing the hypocrites
Who describe such acts as Your judgment
Against us, "the new Sodom"),
Instead of turning to You for solace.
Or wisdom.
And longer vision.
But I can see already
Some positive fallout from these horrors:
More people are praying,
Even daring to be seen in the act;
More people are running to You, Daddy God,
Looking for salvation from the unbearable
(Grant them, I ask,
A hungrier heart
To learn about the salvation
That matters for eternity);
More people are willing
To hold the hands they used to spit on—
To get help or, more's the beauty, to give;
More people are inclined to invoke Your name
With awe and homage
Who used to casually toss it around
Or spew it out as invective;
More have turned from calling down curses,
Asking You instead to bless.

PERSPECTIVE

Do I feel closer to You
Just now
Than ever before?
Yes.
But not for the obvious reasons,
As You know so well.
I have many cherished times
When I have been especially
   close to You,
Just as I have many
   learning times
When I was particularly far,
My back turned
So I could pretend
You had deserted me...
But You know the person I am
   today,
The person I was yesterday,
And the person You created me
   to be tomorrow,
So You know I have been
   drawing closer to You
Ever since I said yes to Your call
Yes to Your hand on my shoulder
Yes, to start a new journey
Yes, to enter a life of ministry.
Ever since, I have needed to draw
   on You
For insight, discernment, more
   stamina,
To accomplish the tasks of study
   and discovery.
I have learned to see You in the
   tiniest glimpses
And in the broadest vistas.
In the moist corner of an eye
And in the warmth of hail-fellow-
   well-met embraces.
Through my morning aches and
   evening yawns.

In the comfort of Your presence
And the challenge of interfacing
With those who would change
   Your résumé.
Continue, I pray, to make me a
   blessing
And to keep me from being a
   burden.
Let me only be an obstacle
   to those
Who need to trip over faith
In order to look up to You.

KIDS

Dear Lord!
We are such children.
We're in such a hurry
To proclaim ourselves grown-ups,
Just so we can tell You
We'll do what *we* want.
We insist on our own way,
Don't we?
Getting into fights
And scrapes
With just about anyone
Who gets in our way.
We don't always do
What is commendable,
Or pure,
Or pleasing
To anyone but ourselves.
Then don't we come crying
To You,
Our ever-loving,
Ever-patient,
Ever-waiting Daddy,
To show You our boo-boos,
To tell You we're sorry,
And to ask You
To make it all better.
And You already have.

October 13

CAUGHT

Lord, we admit it.
We know it.
We often get caught up
In our vain culture.
We want to buy the latest,
Look the best,
Be noticed and admired.
Sometimes we forget:
A successful life isn't about $200 shoes
Or the "right" label on our jeans.
Sometimes we forget:
Gunning it through the yellow light
Isn't an achievement,
It's a danger to others.
Too often we walk blindly
Past the homeless
Pretending they are someone else's litter
Or background color for a movie shoot.
Forgive my poor judgment.
Forgive my improper focus.
Send a jolt to this new heart You've given me.
Allow me to see with Your eyes.
Teach me to love like Your Son,
With arms outstretched
Holding on to nothing but nails.

October 14

HANDS OUT

Lord of the Universe,
We confess that we come to You
With our hands wide open
To take.
Yet often we forget to thank You
For all You give.
Precious Redeemer,
We confess that even if we do
Remember to thank You
For all You give,
We often forget
To tell others about Your love.
Author of Life,
We confess that even if we do
Remember to tell others
About Your love,
We often forget to tell them
We are completely dependent on You
For all we need.
Lord of Hosts,
Forgive me, I pray,
For stumbling and grumbling
In my walk with You.
Help me keep my eyes on my Shepherd,
As He leads me on mountain paths.
And help me,
As I keep one hand open to receive,
To keep the other hand always giving back.

October 15

PLAGUE

In this time of fear
In this time of testing
In this time of epidemic violence,
Terrorism and threats
Of germ warfare, *jihad*,
Famine and fire
In this time of burgeoning
Skirmishes,
Posturing,
Prodding,
Provoking
In this time of uncertain beliefs,
Fast-shift focus,
Shallow roots
In this time of unhappiness,
Heart and soul disease,
Horror and hatred,
Make our joy more contagious,
I pray, than any plague.
Let our joy, which is Your light
Torching out darkness, shine
Let our joy be a beacon
Let our joy summon the suffering
To soothing comfort,
To ease their disease
Let our joy immunize as many
As will pause to bare their hearts
And open their fists.

October 16

SNEAKERS

Listening to footsteps
   today, Lord,
I've seen sneakers with new eyes!
They've become ubiquitous,
Universal,
The soles of our universe.
Like the tires of our pony cars
And monster trucks,
They all have unique treads:
To stick, squeak, turn,
Jump, land, run…
Like everything else
In our post-modern,
Globalized society,
Sneakers are now highly
   specialized:
Tennis shoes
Basketball shoes
Walking, jogging, running shoes
Aerobics and cross-trainers
And a dozen more, I'm sure.
What happened to good
   old Keds?
A little canvas, a little rubber,
Lace 'em up and fly.
And I'm thinking about our
   churches, Lord.
They used to be like sneakers,
Different in color and size, sure,
But no need to specialize
In anything but serving You.
Today there are so many models I
   can't keep track
And I wonder, precious
   Shepherd,
If all that specialization isn't
   serving
The serpent more than You
As we run in separate directions;
As we trash each other's views
On how, where, when and why
   to worship
Or who is fit to serve in
   Your name,
We become more thorns on
   Your brow,
More nails in Your hands.

October 17

FRAGMENTS

When You join two people in marriage,
The two become one whole,
So if they break themselves apart,
They are no longer complete individuals,
I heard someone say today,
But rather halves of the whole.
And isn't it true, Lord,
That some of us are so abused
By society, or family, or life,
That we feel fragmented,
Broken, shattered into jagged bits,
And we yearn for wholeness.
We look, sometimes desperately,
For someone to fit our emptiness,
To fill our cracks, mend our shards,
Smooth our painful edges.
How foolish we are, running headlong
Into walls that smash us into ruin,
Yet all the while our healing waits,
Master Potter,
In Your sweet, warm, welcoming hands.

CHAOS

When people admire my orderliness
I have to laugh, Lord,
Because You and I know
How chaotic I am by nature,
How laissez-faire at home
(At least until company comes,
Or I remember You are always there).
The giggles erupt,
Sputtering,
Splattering joyful peals
At the silly irony—
Just like my spontaneous
Riot of laughter
In this morning's traffic
When a speedster
Shoved his way in and out of lanes
With self-important urgency
Only to lose, a short time later,
Ten times the five feet he had gained…
The ultimate lesson,
God of the universe,
Is always that without You
Order is artificially imposed
On the chaos of our fallen world,
And cannot survive
The drive toward entropy.

CREATIVITY

Any look around the house
Any walk through the workplace
Every street and highway,
City block, strip mall, parking lot...
The evidence of human creativity
Is completely inescapable.
Planes in the sky
Radio stations, TV, websites,
Satellite dishes, cell phones,
Books, paintings, statues,
Banners, signs, traffic lights—
Lord, everywhere I go,
Everything I do,
Reminds me of our ingenuity
And accomplishment,
But also reminds me, Lord,
That we are made in Your image,
You who are the first and only God;
You who are the first and only Creator of all;
You who gave us imagination,
Intelligence, vision and the courage to wish;
You who gave us the dexterity to fashion
The things we dream.

ON CLOUDS

Inverted mountains of pewter and steel
Hang over the horizon
As far as I can see
A looming menace
This range rises downward
Heavy with impending rain.
Only the occasional glint of crimson dawn
Brightens the view
(Although I remember "Red sky
In the morning, sailors take warning!")
And as I mull over my checklist
For rain gear and storm contingency plans,
You remind me, Lord,
In one quick flash,
That the weather we call "threatening"
Is Your water bearer to a thirsty world.
So I relax
I thank You
And I take the time to admire
The breathtaking beauty
And infinite variety
Of these cloudscapes,
Heaven's aquifer.
May the whole world thirst more
For the One who provides
And less for the one who lies.

AARON'S STAFF

Numbers 17:1-13

I'm not much with history, Lord,
But I figure it was probably
Long past growing season
When You caused Aaron's staff
 to bud,
To bloom
And produce almonds
In just one night,
Lest anyone claim
It was an accident of nature
As modern folk are prone
 to do—
As if nature were independent
As if accidents happen as
 we sleep
As if a hank of wood
Long separated from its root
And drained of sap
Could spontaneously
Produce and sustain
A fragrance of flowers
And a clutch of almonds!
Overnight,
Grumbling turned to fear,
Rebellion to dependence,
Sin to conviction.
You alone are my root and soil,
My sun and rain.
You have chosen me
Like Aaron
Like Moses
To be Your mouthpiece
A leader of thankless renegades
Just like me.
Without You I am dead wood.
Make me bloom, I pray;
Let me bear
Durable, delicious fruit.

October 22

ON FIRE

Humans are a resourceful lot.
You equipped us to create
But we use our vision
To dream up better ways to kill.
You gave us fire:
A gift that warms, gives light,
Cooks food for health and taste;
Yet we use it as an agent
Of revenge and destruction.
Centuries ago, we discovered
The explosive force of gunpowder;
It gave us weapons we could carry
And conceal.
Firearms brought death from a distance.
It felt so good, we continue to perfect
The lethal arts of conveying death:
Bombs, grenades, napalm,
Firepower to the Nth degree.
The violence makes me heartsick,
So I ask, dear Lord—bring
Your hot coals down again
To char and cleanse
Our brains, our lips, our hearts
So that we may no longer hate;
So that we may give up all firearms
And arms of fire for hearts ablaze
With nothing but Your love.

DEUS EX MACHINA

You gave us the earth to tame,
To cultivate, to protect, to grow.
It's a loaner, but we've forgotten;
Being in the driver's seat so long,
It's easy to get carried away
With the hum of her engine,
The squeal of her wheels
As we wait around the turns,
The wind beats at our doors
The crowd roars in our ears
Our hearts pump faster
We ignore the yellow flag
And step on the gas.
Forget the debris, we mutter,
We've got it nailed.
Clear the road of wimps,
Hoist our colors, mark our time.
Not ready for a pit stop.
Change of driver? No way
Things are just getting fun…
What? The official has shut down the track?
The Owner has called in this ride
And all drivers are back to the post?
We climb out of the machine
Toss the key at Your feet
And poke each other
'Cause we're afraid to swipe at You.
We do know, but won't admit,
We've botched the job You gave us…

We cultivated hate where You sowed love,
Built despair on Your foundations of hope,
Hoisted the banner of competition
On Your tree of sacrifice.
As we bow our heads in shame
We humbly ask for another chance
This time, we want You to do the driving.

INTERVIEW

USA Today *asks, "What's your story?"*

Thus says the LORD God:
My children are faithless hypocrites.
They break my heart every day
Yet I will love them always.
I set them aside from others
I gave them unique blessings
I delivered them out of slavery into freedom
I did all the work myself
I provided for their every need
I covered their flaws so I could walk with them,
The Holy among the unholy *rendered* holy...
Still, my children are thankless brats.
They run to me, clamoring, crying, begging, pleading,
But when I give them what they need
They complain it's not what they want,
And if I give them what they want
They grumble *Not enough! Wrong kind!*
My children are self-centered hellions.
Even when they talk about me
It's only in terms of what they get.
When I am with them, they ignore
Or accuse me; when I am gone,
They forget or insult me.
All but a faithful few, that is,
Who truly love me and my boy,
Who understand their own role
In this world and the next,
And who take the time to say
Thanks, Dad. You're the best!

THIS MORNING

This morning
I was a victim of sun glare
And human stupidity.
Perhaps that is cruel;
I should say obstinacy.
Foolishness. Ignorance.
Or sheepishness,
For they follow yesterday's
Patterns and react to predictable
Trials with panic—
As though sunrise
Were totally unexpected.
I watched precious minutes
Tick away; I saw the road
Empty ahead, beyond the unprepared,
The paralyzed drivers,
Useless before the blinding light.
Then I realized, Lord,
How a sudden revelation
Of Your might, Your holiness,
Your grace, Your love, Your mercy…
A sudden blast of Your Light,
Stops me dead in my tracks
As I shield my eyes
And scramble to absorb
The magnitude of Your glory.

PULSE

You've taught me, Lord,
As I sing Your praises
In metric rhythm,
As I read Your Word
With rising or falling accent
And those important pauses;
As I observe our world
And ponder the universe...
You've taught me, Lord,
To hear and feel the throb of life:
The regular pattern of calm breaths;
The beat of every timepiece,
Manmade or otherwise;
Cosmic motion, seasons and tides,
Sound waves and light,
Cycles and phases all around.
As You gather me into Your hand
I feel the pulse that drives creation,
And as You draw me to Your breast
I recognize all music is composed
To the beat of Your heart.

ILLUMINATION

Under the incandescent bulb
That chased the shadows
This winter morning
A burgundy turtleneck
Seemed the perfect match
For my shades of purple
Color-blocked sweater.
But in the bright sunlight
It fights the lilac, wine and plum,
Hurts like the proverbial thumb,
And I see the error of my ways:
Human illumination
Is but a dim imitation
Of what You alone can reveal.

October 28

NIGHT WATCH

The nights are cold.
The air bites shrewdly,
As Shakespeare wrote,
And each time I stir,
I realize the cats have me pinned
Under the quilt and flannel sheet,
Like tent pegs in the desert
Or weights on a picnic cloth.
They warm me on either side.
They comfort me with the rhythm
And rumble of their purring snores.
I feel their pressure even before I wake
And I am reminded, Lord,
Of Your presence,
Your protection, Your comfort.
You are my anchor
Against the riptide.
You are my guard
Against the chill
And the other perils of night.

SABBATICAL

Deuteronomy 15:1

What would happen, Lord,
To our capitalist domain
If we obeyed Your law of the Sabbath year
And, every seventh calendar cycle,
We forgave ALL debts,
Freed ALL slaves,
Rested the fields and forests?
What would happen, I wonder,
If every seventh year we melted
All weapons of war and destruction
Transforming them instead
Into tools of peace and cultivation?
What if we embraced our enemies?
Or just held hands instead of drawing guns?
What would happen, I ponder,
If we gave each other a Sabbath year
A total break from alienation?
From belittling, from enslavement?
From self-righteous condemnation?
What would happen, I pray, Lord,
If we declared a world amnesty
On human hate
For just one year?

HEALING

Lord, I have been wanting to ask You
To strike the word *hatred* from human tongues,
To remove all cognates around the world:
All nouns, all verbs, all adjectives and such.
It was an attractive theory, You see.
If we had no way to name it,
Maybe we'd forget how to feel it.
But then I remembered Mrs. Brooks
Who taught us, with a quick sine curve
Chalked on the board, there are no peaks
Without valleys, no peaches without pits.
We need to know the meaning of sin
To grasp Your gift of grace.
We need to know the impact of hate
To ache for Your healing love.

October 31

AMBUSH

At the red light
A sudden sharp rap
Like a rock projected
Against my window—
And I snap
Up left to see
A ferocious face
A mere glass width away:
Satan with a scrubby beard.
Where'd You learn to drive?
He growls,
His voice stabbing
Grabbing my throat
Through the barely open pane
Then he runs back to his Honda
One lane over, behind,
And I think
As my heart jams hip hop
Where'd You come from?
Why terrorize me? What'd I do?
I rewound the tape,
Saw myself hit the brakes
And blare the horn at a
    reckless kid
What could that possibly mean
    to him?

Perhaps my offense was
    making noise
Perhaps it was the sin of the kid
    visited on me
Perhaps the real scandal is not
    how I drive
But where I am headed…
I breathe a prayer of thanks
For the mostly closed window
And a strong heart,
Shift into first and drive on
To the seminary
Where I learn more about
    serving
The One who has conquered
    the knave
That sent this errand boy.
Where do You think You're going?
He might have snarled.
I know where I'm going.
And unlike those who think
    they're gods,
I know I am not the Driver.

November 1

ORAL EXAM

We are obsessed with what goes in our mouths:
We eat, we snack, we nibble,
We cram, we feast, we taste;
We think with a finger, a toothpick,
A pen, a straw between our teeth,
Pressed against our lips;
We drink, we gulp, we sip…
We are obsessed with what goes in our mouths
Yet we pay little heed to what goes out:
The faint praise
The caustic remark
The biting phrase
The offputting bark
The downputting sting.
The mouth You gave us to speak praise,
To encourage, counsel, love, amuse,
We use indiscriminately to offend,
Insult, slight, diminish, wound, abuse.
Forgive us, Lord. Sew up our lips,
Until we are able to taste the acrid
Poison we spew so freely;
Until we burn with shame
Until we spurn the barbs
Until we leave the nasties on the altar
And beg pardon of those we've harmed.

THE NEWS

For Betty: poet, sister, friend.

Some news is welcome, some news is not;
Some news recycles, some news is hot;
Most news is heralded, but some is hushed;
At some news we blanch, with others we blush;
Some news brings joy, others cause tears;
Some news stirs boldness, others bring fears.
Headlines are often ambiguous, unintentionally so;
Reports are subjective, no matter what they intend;
Sometimes imagination rewrites as we read alone;
Then we run screaming the half-truths we apprehend.
When we start feeling shell-shocked or cringe in despair,
Dear Lord, remind us--whisper in our ear or rock the air--
That we belong to You, heart, body, mind and soul;
Nothing and no one can harm us; in You we are whole.
Journals, doctors, media may cry out along the road,
"Bad news! Disaster! Woe to all! We're going to die!"
But their energy is wasted, as many already know,
The Good News is through Jesus we have eternal life.

SALT

Lot's wife looked back.
You warned them not to,
But Lot's wife looked back.
Regret? Curiosity? Defiance?
You said, *Don't!* and she did.
Lot's wife looked back,
And You turned her into salt.
A pillar of salt.
And I'm wondering, Lord,
Why *salt*?
The most precious commodity
Of their time and place...
Not stone, a monument to human will...
Not sand, lasting yet ever shifting in winds...
Not wood, consumed as You torched their town...
Lot's wife looked back,
And You turned her into salt:
A fortune of regret for Lot
Who lost home, wife and wealth
All at once,
But gained life,
Because he was a righteous man;
Because he obeyed Your command.

November 4

WAR

Zephaniah 3:1-20 & Revelation 12:1-18

The words You sent me as I tried to sleep,
As the dishwasher churned;
Your words were clear,
Their delivery fearsome;
Your words were clear,
But elusive in meaning.
I heard them proclaimed
Solo by a dark male voice,
Then in duet with an alto,
Building to crescendo
Along the percussive beat
As a heroic chorus joined in.
Doom? Judgment? Retribution?
Chanted my brain as
My heart pounded in synch;
What about grace, Lord?

How do I hear this message?
Your words grew louder,
Clearer still; I feared
My heart might stop
As I felt the words
Etch a record in my mind:
"All is decided.
War is declared.
All is decided.
War is declared.
All is decided:
War is declared!
War is declared!
War is declared!"
I'm frightened, Lord,
But send me to the front.

PLAINT

Plaint or plainsong
We seem to waffle between
Whine and worship
Loud and laud
Snotty and sublime
You are so gracious, Lord God,
Such a loving Parent
Patient with Your unruly kids;
Thank You for Your mercy,
Your even temper,
Your long-suffering smile
As we cry at Your feet
With clenched teeth or fists,
Your gentle reproof,
Your hand raised in blessing
Rather than wrath.

November 6

REFOCUS

It's November and the morning light is diffused
By impenetrable fog to a bruise-like blued amber;
The fiery leaves have banked to faded embers,
Yet the forsythia are in full bloom again.
The cats have donned their winter coats,
The bed is comforted in quilts and flannel,
The heat registers tick regularly into the silence,
Yet the forsythia are in full bloom again.
The hunter's moon was nearly full last night,
Spooky graveyard displays make room for
Turkeys, Pilgrims, pumpkins and corn,
Yet the forsythia are in full bloom again.
Wood smoke, pressed apples, fresh bread and pies
Fill the air with sweet promise, beckoning us
To the harvest table to give thanks,
While the forsythia are in full bloom again.
Even the seasons of life are confused
While we make war, terrorize the terrified
And label them terrorists; all creation groans
As the cancer of human contempt grows
And spreads its death. But You are our hope,
Cherished Lord, as You remind us
As the forsythia are in full bloom again.

POW!

In a recent film, a coal miner's son
Is consumed with the need to dance
He explodes into motion
At the slightest provocation
Sometimes joyful, sometimes pained
By the intensity of his gift.
"It's like electricity," he says,
Unable to express otherwise in words
This power that impels him to leap,
To thrust his limbs about, to soar
In tension between heaven and earth.
His dance is what poetry is to me.
The creative gifts You give us, Lord,
The ardent fires that smolder,
Waiting for a waft of air,
Are all like electricity:
We need You to provide the charge.
A zing from outside in, it jolts
Our body, heart, mind and spirit,
Travels through and seeks ground beyond.
Pow!
Keep me plugged in, dear Lord,
And let me sizzle and glow;
May the words I write always dance,
Drawing eyes to You, their source.

November 8

YOUR WOMEN

Lord God, there is so much controversy
In Your church today about the role of women.
But when we look back,
We realize there always has been.
From the very beginning,
You have revealed Yourself to women as to men,
And You have given spiritual gifts to both,
According to Your purposes,
Not ours.
We are unspeakably grateful, Lord,
For the privilege of being called
To praise and worship You,
To nurture Your children,
To serve You and our neighbors,
With love and humility,
To teach, and, when You put the words
In our mouths, to preach,
Whether it is at our kitchen table,
In the meeting places of our community,
Or in more officially recognized positions.
Above all, gracious and loving God,
We thank You for the work
You are doing to unite Your church universal,
To use us *and* our brothers,
Our husbands, our fathers, our sons,
To break down the walls that split Your people.
Continue to guide us.
Open our ears, our eyes, our hearts
To discern Your will.
Use us in a mighty way, dear Lord,
To further Your kingdom
And to prepare the way for Your return.
As much as we cheer *vive la différence*,
We also look forward to an eternal life
When difference will no longer divide.

BUFFETED

Stop Your shoving, Lord, keep Your hands
To Yourself—I can barely stand!
Ever since I left the house You've been at me:
Push, push, push, this way, that way, You bat me
Like a cat its toy. With all due respect, how
Am I supposed to keep my little car in its place now
At 65 miles an hour forward while You blow
Us broadside at 40? It's hard enough, You know,
To keep clear of the kamikaze rushing my flanks
And now I have to watch heaven, too? Thanks
A lot, Lord; I thought You were on my side…
What's that? Excuse me? I'm being "snide"?
Treating You like what? Taking You for granted?
Oh, and I was out of line, so to speak, when I ranted
At the driver who kept crawling up my tailpipe?
But—
Oh.
No,
I see.
Somehow I got upside down in my view of life;
Your wind tipped me over, stood me on my head,
Reminded me that it shouldn't just be times of strife
That bring me to the throne of God. Instead
Today and every day hence, I pray,
Be my God, keep me meek, lest I stray.

BENCHES

Some benches are hard
Unyielding
Austere
They seem to say,
"Park it here,
But don't plan to stay!"
Armless or not
With a back or without
Dished or flat
Or pitched toward the door.
Some benches are cushioned
With pillows plump or lean.
Some are weathered
By use, abuse and neglect,
Others are polished to reflect
Hours of care
A sense of class
And expectations.
Benches are inviting
Though never quite cozy.
How like Your children, dear God!
Most of us are polite and welcoming
Until we are sat upon…

STARTING FIRES

Most smokers toss burning butts
Wherever they happen to be
When necessary becomes nuisance.
Heedless of hazards,
Careless of consequence,
Willfully oblivious to others,
They dump the litter and walk on
With abandon, as the spark lingers
Until a willing wind lifts it against
Other refuse and rubbish,
Dry tinder, tasty fuel for greedy flames.
I watch one more smoky stub fly
And realize yet again, Lord,
How recklessly we all disregard
Your creation, Your creatures,
Your commands that we cultivate
This planet, that we be wardens,
Wise, not wasteful destroyers
Of what Your hand has provided.
Let me be a firebrand, Lord,
Solely under Your direction,
To work Your purpose
And to douse discarded embers.

November 12

PREACHING TO THE CHOIR

This morning I was thinking, Lord,
How the phrase *preaching to the choir*
Is supposed to mean a waste of time,
Energy better spent elsewhere,
The assumption being that the singers
Who lead worship with joy and zeal
Are first among Your fold.
And I realized, Lord, what fools
We are to leap to conclusions
And proclaim "self-evident truths".
Only You know each human heart
And the state of each human soul;
Only You know the sheep
From the fleece-clad wolves.
We can never proclaim Your gospel
Too plainly or too often;
I'll delete this foolish figure
From my storehouse.
And even if they sit behind me,
I'll keep preaching to the choir.

SURPRISED

Lord, You know I was exasperated
As I sputtered, wondering again today
Why drivers, as they come round
Each curve that they drive every day,
Are so surprised
By the rising sun
That they jam their brakes,
Unable see the road ahead.
Then You said to me,
"It's exactly the same way
Most live with my Word,
Forgetting over and over
That what I say will be
Will be."
Like the sun You bring us
Every morning, Lord,
Your Word is a torch to the dark.
You have mapped the road,
And You offer to pilot our way.
Forgive us, Lord, when we fail
To heed Your voice;
Pardon us when we forget
To shield ourselves in You,
And fall prey to the blinding glare,
The false light of sin.

November 14

HAMMOCK

On a lazy summer day,
I am suspended on a nylon sling;
My canopy is like a Mummer's
 multi-leveled dress,
Wide swaths of maple leaves,
Rustling, swooshing, flapping
As the breezes flirt through their
 individual skirts;
When the wind jumps up a notch
They shimmy and shake,
Flap and snap and slap each
 other.
The leaves are not just green.
The sun is high, peering down
Through this curtain of lace,
These insect-pierced five-pointed
Sheets, opaque or translucent,
Depending on their place.
Some are a new grass lime shade,
Some lighter, like Oriental jade.
Others are emerald, or sea glass
 green.
The sun seems a distant light
Behind, above this giant tree
That cools me in its shadow
And mesmerizes me
With its branch ballet.
And I thank You, Lord God,
Creator of trees,
Mover of leaves;
Invisible wind,
You make Yourself known
Through all my senses.
You provide all my needs
And add the joy, the miracle,
Of nature, to tickle me,
To rouse me from my book
To give You spontaneous praise!

YIELD

How could we forget, Lord?
We see it on signs every day
Yet we behave as if convinced
Those signs are for everyone but us.
We've distorted our world
To such an extent that Yield
Has only one meaning now:
How much do I get?
How perverse we are!
We turn everything inside out
Upside down and backwards.
Teach us again, dear God,
To yield to You,
For until we do,
We cannot yield to others;
We can only succumb to base desires,
Surrendering our souls in the bargain.
Teach us again, dear God,
To yield to You.
Let us learn to ask
How much may I give?

November 16

VAPORIZED

Early morning fog clouds the mountain
Or perhaps it is a cloud that fogs the way,
Down and around the precarious descent.
Two hours pass and, traveling back,
The mist is now rising
As, awesome sight! shafts of sunlight
Pierce the steel sky,
Like slats of vertical blinds
And there
Everywhere
Suspended in mid-air
Dancing in the sunbeams
Are millions of tiny particles,
Dust and water,
Rising like bubbles
And I find myself praising You, Lord,
For the sun and the rain,
For this beautiful sight
You have placed upon my path
And for the sudden realization
That the image I see is a symbol
A metaphor
For our relationship with You.
We are dust and water
Molded together by Your hand
And held, by Your grace,
In suspension
Between earth and heaven.
We cannot rise on our own merits
We cannot power our own journey
And unless we follow Your light
Through the overhanging darkness,
We will diffuse
Dissipate
Evaporate
Like morning fog.

MURDER MOST FOUL

It lays heavy on my heart, Lord.
My friend's wife Bathsheba
Swore her undying love
Then sent him off to war,
To bear Your banner
On the mission front.
And while he was gone
David the trusted leader
The speaker of Your truth
The shepherd of Your flock
Desired her
Wooed her
Seduced her
And made her his own.
No need to send the order
To murder Uriah in the field;
His knees buckled
With the weight of the sword
Plunged deep into his back.

It lays heavy on my heart, Lord.
My friend's wife Gertrude
Swore her undying love
As she plotted with Claudius,
His brother in faith,
To change allegiance
And move her bed;
So Claudius came upon him,
Noble, naive King Hamlet,
Napping in the garden
Where he had come to plant.
Vulnerable in his openness,
Now slain by his once-trusted
   brother.

CHAPEL AT HYDEPARK

Doorn, the Netherlands

Lord, You are the musical creak of the wooden bench
The flame slowly consuming the center pillar of ivory wax
The multi-hued stones imbedded in the concrete floor
The sienna grid of the rusted grating
The green leaves and honey-colored flowers strewn
In the shape of a Celtic cross
The gentle fall of incoming feet
The quiet sighs of prayerful souls
The birds singing unfamiliar songs in the thicket
Beyond angled panes of clear glass
The rain-filled sky
The wet grass
The flute
The organ
The lilt of our voices in worshipful song
The prayers
The tears
Lord, You are the breath, the voice, the heart
And the object of our praise.

published in **The Church Herald**, November 2003.

November 19

ENGINEERING A CLOSER LOOK

Doorn, the Netherlands

Human construct is a scaffolding
Used in attempts to rise to a place
Where we will find the voice
The image
The words
Of God...
Why do we climb on our own?
We do not speak fluently
The language of God,
So we feel drawn
To stick our hands
Into the unfathomable,
Propped up,
Even propelled
By our own platforms.

UNCOMFORTABLE SILENCE

Doorn, the Netherlands

The uncomfortable silence in chapel
The waiting for someone to speak
Or music to flow, to spill out, to fill the void,
To drown our awkward discomfort...
Later we will read Wiesel and other voices
On the impenetrable silence of people
Confronted by human evil...

No space is devoid of You, Lord God.
The silence is unbearable
Because we cannot hide from Your overwhelming presence
There is judgment and wrath, mercy and grace,
Fury and love.
How like You we are, Lord.
Fury and love.

WE WERE THERE

Doorn, the Netherlands

In the time-honored ritual of Pesach
We remind each other to tell the story
As though we ourselves were slaves in Egypt
Redeemed by God
As though we ourselves walked out of bondage
Across the wilderness
To freedom
And to become servants of God.

I believe we are all,
Whether born Jews or spliced into Israel
By faith in Messiah,
We are all
Called to tell the story of Shoah
As though we were there
In the deportation centers
In the trains
In the death camps
In the gas chambers
In the ovens
We must all struggle with human evil
And the presence
Or perceived absence
Of God.

published online at www/uugreensboro.org in October 2003 and in **The Church Herald**, November 2003.

ABANDONED

Gouda, the Netherlands

Childhood fear
Groundless, fanciful trauma
Unreasonable terror
All three descend
Like a cage
As I step out of the toilet—
Filthy and paperless—
In this foreign station
And find myself alone.
My friends, my classmates,
My fellow travelers this day
My dinner companions
Gone.
Evaporated.
I feel abandoned.
Not just alone
But cast off.
Not forgotten—
They were just there!
I run to find the next train
Scour the platform
Perhaps they've gone ahead
The scoundrels
Complicit in this odd plot
To leave me behind
Yet once on the train

A sudden fear of another sort,
A guilty shroud:
I think
What if they're searching that station
For me
Now I've gone missing
Now I've abandoned them,
The faithful,
Who may have just stepped away
At the wrong moment
And I judged them so unfairly!
Should I return?
No, I'll make amends on arrival,
I decide.

In the end, I find several are already
Relaxing at home.
"Oh, hi!" they say,
As though nothing has happened.

Yet, instead of anger,
Suddenly I feel the panic
The angst
The terror
Of others
Who would have fared better
If just abandoned
But were instead
Loaded on trains
Crammed
Into filthy, paperless holes
And carted off
Like lambs to the slaughter.

THIS CROSS IS YELLOW WITH SIX POINTS

Doorn, the Netherlands

This pain I feel is not rightfully mine, LORD,
Yet I wince, I tremble, I want to pull away.
This slaughter did not touch my family
Yet I shudder, I quake, I feel faint.
These millions of souls
Stripped of their rights
Stripped of their goods
Stripped of their clothes
Stripped of their dignity
Stripped of their skin, LORD—
They were not my forebears
Yet I weep, I wail silent screams
That fall to the ground like shards of glass
And ring back to Your ears, O LORD.
I am wrung out.
I am crammed in a boxcar—
I am unable to breathe, to move, to whimper.
I am vaporized up a smokestack
And my now grey blood marks a thin line
Against Your brooding brow.
I died six million times, LORD,
In hidden forests, places with unspeakable names
Now known to all…

And I die again
Every day
Because the ovens are still hot
Because the camp cots are still full
Because the boxcars still transport their loads.
Human loathing was the first successful clone;
"Different" continues to mean hated,
Expendable.
Alas, blood still calls for blood.
When *Your* blood was shed, Lord,
It should have been enough.
It should have been enough.

Will we never realize, dear God,
No other bodies need be broken?
No other blood—
No *more* blood—
Should be spilled.
You alone are sufficient.
You alone.

published in **The Church Herald**, November 2003.

DRIEBERGEN

Driebergen, the Netherlands

On such days as we have seen
When rain unites pewter skies
And mud-rimmed tin streets
When clouds lay heavy and obvious
As drunken belches
Like smoke and ash
Wafted over farmlands from factory stacks
I wonder how many
Who once walked these streets
And labored in these fields
Are now feeding the roots of others' crops
Just a few hours away.

Who remembers you?
Who mourns you still?
Who tells your life, your joys, your everyday sorrows?
Who sings your particular song?
Who speaks your name
To defy the machine that ground you down
And burned you into charcoal
For a failed artist's scribble on history?

November 25

ON MONUMENTS

People need monuments, Lord.
We need our senses to be engaged
When we remember the great or
   the horrid
To focus our attention
To widen or narrow perspective
To overcome distraction
To occupy our physical selves
So our spirit and soul may reflect
Concentrate
Meditate
In meaningful ways.
How well You know us, dear Lord,
Our limitations and our excesses.
Thank You for instructing us
Concerning the building of altars
   to You,
To keep us from sanctifying the
   mundane.
Thank You for commanding us
Concerning ritual celebrations
Of Your powerful
   outstretched arms
And concerning the
   remembrance of human acts
Whether of malice or love.
We learn to order our steps
By looking backward
By scanning ahead
By poking around at our
   current state
But most of all
By reading Your Word
Holding it in our heart
Cherishing its truth
Day in, day out
And age to age…

Let me be a monument,
I pray, while I am here,
That others may see,
Hear and feel You in me
That they may crave a taste
For themselves,
Then stay to feast at Your table.

REMEMBERING

Praise the LORD,
Who remembers all people,
Faithful and unfaithful alike.
Praise the LORD,
Who remembers all promises,
Given and received,
God's covenants, human
    obligations.
Praise the LORD,
Who gave us memory:
The capacity to store and recall
For our pleasure
For our leisure
For our education
And edification;
Stories to tell our children
And children's children;
Stories to tell the nations,
Promises to cherish,
Duties to perform,
Forgiveness to remember,
Sins to forgive and forget.
Praise the LORD,
Who mourns human evil,
Who soothes and heals our
    wounds,
Who knows every freckle on
    our face,
Every step and stumble of
    our feet;
Who delights in our conversation
Even when we whine.
Praise the LORD,
Who remembers all people!

published in October 2003 on http://www.uugreensboro.org/news_and_views.html

November 27

HELL

Suffering has many shapes;
And it comes in all sizes,
Though even the smallest
Is far too large.
Suffering has many names:
Violence, torture,
Famine, plague,
Injustice, bigotry,
Accident or not…
Our favorite metaphor
For suffering is *hell on earth*.
It was Sartre, I remember,
Who wrote, "Hell is other people."
Today I am thinking of those
Unhappy fortunate few
Who survive a global horror
And must continue their lives
Under the shadow
Under the burden
Of *why me* guilt.
It is a monster,
This *angst*
That lurks
In the minds,
Hearts and spirits,
Under the skin,
In every corner,
Behind every door,
On every breath
Every second
Of every new day
For the unfortunate fortunate,
These incomplete victims
Who must meet each sunrise
With a prayer of thanksgiving
And a prayer of woe,
To have known what they know
To have seen what they see
To have felt what they feel.
How I pray, dear Lord,
That all victims of human sin
May come to You, precious Savior,
For only Your living water
Can quench the fires of hell.

November 28

GIVING THANKS

Just a week ago today, Lord, we gathered as a nation
To give thanks.
We thanked our families, we thanked our friends,
We thanked our neighbors,
And remembered to thank our employers.
And *most* of us took time to thank You...
Tonight, Lord, we thank You.
For all Your blessings:
You cause the sun to shine and the rain to fall on all,
Whether they know You or not.
Tonight, Lord, we thank You.
For Your mercy and Your grace.
Tonight, Lord, we thank You.
For Your infinite patience,
For Your willingness to forgive us,
for Your sacrifice, that we might be saved.
Tonight, Lord, we look ahead to Advent,
The time of Your coming to earth as a human child.
The time You set aside Your glory to walk among us.
The time You stepped out of eternity to live within time.
Tonight, Lord, we look ahead to Easter,
The perfect ending to the perfect story of our redemption.
We look forward to the day when everyone will thank You
With a glad heart and a full knowledge that You are Lord.

November 29

IRONY OF IRONIES

Lord of creation, Shepherd of my heart,
You know all things;
You are the architect who plumbs true;
You hear the questions that plague me,
You see the distress caused by what I observe,
You must feel conflicted, I reason,
By the ironic separation
Between You and Your children
Caused by the gift You chose to give!
If we had not the free will to choose,
If we had not the imagination to dream,
If we lacked the capacity for envy and greed,
If we were impervious to the tempter's lure,
If we hungered for You alone,
There would be no idols,
There would be no strife,
No rage, no anguish,
No victims, no crime.
We would have no words to speak
Of theft, abuse, rape or murder,
No way to name what could not exist:
Embezzlement, tyranny, terror, lies;
Ethnic cleansing, calumny, revenge,
All human sacrifices on the altar of evil.
We are deeply flawed by this gift You gave;
It blinds us to the greater Gift and the healing
Bridge He built through—O irony again!—
Human hatred, envy, betrayal and lies.
Lord of lords and King of kings,
You are Riddle of riddles, Irony of ironies.

WRONGS

As we prepare to start the
    church year anew
With the Advent of our Lord;
As we put aside the pumpkins,
    Pilgrims and paper turkey
    cutouts
And get out the angels,
    shepherds and manger scenes,
It is time to reflect once again on
    the greatness of our God.
The grandeur of God's plan for
    humanity.
The amplitude of God's love and
    grace.
I find myself thinking:
Because God's mercy put Jesus
    on the cross for each of us,
Because God's forgiveness
    brought Jesus out of the tomb,
Because God's promise will bring
    Jesus back to earth in glory,
Humanity's petty squabbles are
    an insult to God,
The way children's playing with
    matches and burning down
    the house
Is an insult to their parents'
    hard work and painstaking
    instruction.
Our wastefulness,
Our competitive streak,
Our tendency to point fingers of
    disgust
And to turn backs of distrust on
    those who are different,
These all break God's heart and
    add thorns to Christ's crown.
Should we despair because even
    the redeemed
Are often unrepentant,
    degenerate sinners
Who would rather tear each
    other down
Than build up the kingdom of God?
Sometimes I cry for less.
But then God reminds me
We are all works in progress,
And it is only the Creator,
    Redeemer and Sanctifier
Who has eyes keen enough to
    see our flaws
And hands steady enough to
    fix them.
Our job is to praise, to thank, to
    worship God,
And to be Christ to each other,
    no matter what.

December 1

ENFOLD

O God, have You forgotten Israel?
Her enemies encamp around her!
They ravage her market squares!
Stone is ripped from stone,
Bone is torn from bone;
Her cry is, "Woe are we!
Where is our Deliverer?
Where is our mighty God,
Who brought us out of slavery,
Who brought us out of bondage,
Who brought us home from exile,
With a mighty hand
And an outstretched arm?
The beast breaks through
    our gates
And devours our children
Before our helpless,
Horrified eyes.
We make peace with liars,
Who trample our flag of truce
And burn our treaties
To torch our homes.
Where is Adonai,
God of Abraham, Isaac and Jacob,
Our mazel, our shalom?"
Have You turned a deaf ear
To Israel, Your beloved?

She has been unfaithful,
It is true.
But didn't You know her heart
When You first professed
    Your love?
Don't turn Your back, LORD God.
Renew Your covenant,
As You have so many times past;
Stand with Your children
    once more!
Stand and hold firm
Against the eternal evil
That wants her crushed,
Annihilated,
Obliterated,
Eradicated,
Erased from human history.
Come enfold Israel once again
In Your loving embrace!

Then—dare I ask more?
When she is once again
Set safely upon Your hill,
Touch the heart, O God,
Of Ishmael's kin, that they will
Thirst for You, not Israel's blood.

A DADDY PSALM

I'm writing You, Lord, because
    You know where he is,
My sweet, stubborn Daddy,
The armchair reformer
The prophet of doom
Who ignored You but had plenty
    to preach!
You know, Lord, how ardently I
    prayed
That You'd catch him at
    departure,
Reveal Yourself, and humble his
    heart;
So I do trust now that he's
    with You,
Savoring the slow discovery
Of Your many mysteries!
In a moment of calm,
Please send a messenger
To tell him this:

Dear Dad, you may be too busy
To pay much mind to the world
That once consumed your time
And ignited your ire…
And you never were one
To stay long on the phone,
So let me tell you straight away
That thing you quite like to hear:
You were right.
You were right, Dad,
*Atlas is shrugging all over the
    place,*
Just as you griped—and now I
Throw up my hands in disgust,
And wonder
What can we do to get that guy
To do his job, at least as long
As the earth is meant to rest
On his shoulders and in his care?

CHESS

We cry, we scream,
We laugh, we weep,
We make so much noise, Lord,
We can't hear Your voice.
We moan, we groan,
We demand, we deal,
We lie, we sulk,
We wheedle, we steal,
We apologize, we duck…
We are so busy micromanaging
We are oblivious to the truth
If we would only be still
Be still and be willing
Be willing to know
That I AM is God
And God has everything tied up
Planned and plotted out
We are not pawns,
But we are not kings yet either.
Until we cede power to You,
The One who wrote the rules,
It's check
And *mate*
And that means *death*.

GRACE

"Oh, God!" she exclaims. "Jesus Christ!"
A moment later, "I mean, GOD!"
My head snaps up each time,
From saying grace over lunch,
Concerned for the apparent anguish
Causing this diner to invoke Your name
So fervently, so insistently.
But she is only expressing surprise
At the latest news shared by her friend.
"God is here, dear lady," I want to say.
"Jesus is standing near. Turn Your eyes,
Open Your heart, call him gently.
No need to scream God's name
As if it were an expletive or a curse.
Hush a moment. Listen. *Listen!*
Can't You hear the Lord speak *Your* name
In an intimate, urgent whisper of love?
Rather speak God's name with reverence.
With awe. With respect, and praise.
His name is cherished above all names,
Not a trampoline to launch histrionics!
When You invoke God Almighty,
And the Lord of the Universe,
Be ready, dear lady,
To stop Your gossip,
Drop those chopsticks,
And sink to your knees,
For you are in the presence of holiness
Stopping beside you to bestow
A blessing of grace.

RUNNING AHEAD

Traffic on the highway slows down:
Flashing yellow lights are coming
Up the other side... Now we see,
It's an Oversize Load trailer
And its follow car. Oh, and there,
Far ahead, is the lead car,
Running so far ahead
There is no apparent connection
Between them, other than the lights.
And I wonder what possible good
The scout is doing for that cargo,
With some twenty vehicles in-between.
And then I wonder how often, Lord,
You send me on a particular path
With a precise role to play,
Yet I get so excited by the environment
Or the skills You have given me
Or the company I keep,
I forget to keep pace with Your will
And run off in my own direction
At my own speed
Leaving Your precious cargo,
Your Word or Your love or Your care,
Dwindling behind.

THANKLESS

Lord, You know how I get!
Ingratitude grates my teeth,
Sends me reeling,
Seething and spluttering,
Red in the face, so I go
Silent
Tuck my hostility
Into indignation,
Then kvetch You deaf
With childish rant.
Our parents taught us
To say please and thank you
So it aggravates me
When people grab and take
What others freely give
Or they claim entitlement
To what they never earned
And I am outraged
When those self-promoters
Fail
The slightest chance
To lend a hand…

And You let me rage on, Lord,
Until my ire is spent
Or spun up into harmless spit
Then
As I catch my breath
And consider whether I need
To start a new diatribe,
As I pause
Silent
You speak
A soft whisper
Peace
Be still
And know that
I AM God…
Thank you, Lord—
I AM speaking to you, Child.
Yes, Lord—
Be still, I say.
Now get to work
Pluck that forest out
Of your own eye already.

WARMTH

Creator God, Lord of the morning,
What a glorious sight today!
All heaven a dark blue-grey coverlet
A quilt of moisture-laden clouds
And at the very tip, where
One might see a ribbon ticking
On a blanket, there was the edge
Of a freshly laundered
Bright white sheet
So inviting, so sweet,
This line of sunlight
Celebrating the new day.
Thank you, dear God,
For turning down the covers
And tucking us in for the night
And thank you for this gentle
Embrace that invites us
To linger awhile
To feast in Your presence
To button You around us
Before we step out
Into the dangerous cold.

December 8

POWER

The ice is beautiful in the moonlight;
Like December decorations
It coats the November trees,
It pings the bedroom panes
And tinkles as the wind walks by.
Around midnight, the gentle breeze takes a turn, scales up
And bellows from house to house.
The gentle rain is now in hard freeze,
The sharp pellets slam the shingles.
As the heavy limbs rake the roofs
And rap the windows, the trees
Creak. Crack. Groan. Snap,
Like taut live wires, and crash.
I am cold under the quilts
And cats
In the dark
That is filled with the warlike noise
Of nature's assault.
I plague You with ceaseless prayer
Throughout the sleepless night:

Protect us, Lord! Bless this house!
Keep us covered, deflect the trees,
Canopy my friends and neighbors,
Calm my fears...
Thank You, Lord, I found the flashlight,
Thank You, Lord, the roof still holds
At 3 in the morning, on this,
My fourth round, room to room.

Forty hours later, with light, heat
And water finally restored,
Calls made and friends safe,
I can reflect more clearly
On the abject terror, the passive
Resignation, the stoic acceptance
That power comes and goes,
Control is momentary,
And You and You alone are God.

AFTER THE STORM

I don't know why
The ice storm dropped a tree on my roof
I don't know why
The gentle branches hit first to break the fall
I don't know why
Some neighbors have gaping holes
While others only small debris
I don't know why
The pagan neighbor who hates me for my faith
Took it upon herself to summon men she knows
And to tour the property with them,
Pointing out with grave concern even the smallest
Limbs, dangling like unfinished speech
I don't know why
Because I don't know Your detailed plan
But I know that You are Master of my life
And whatever happens
To, around and through me
Is under Your watchful eye
And Your loving hand
So I am very grateful, Lord God,
Even as the tree remains leaning on the house.
You have removed greater obstacles
Far deeper damage
And made me whole.

HALLELUJAH TREES

However gnarled
Twisted
Knotted
Or bent,
Whether thick or thin
Young, middling or ancient,
Their bare arms reach up
And unadorned fingers
Stretch, splayed, to dance
Before You, oh Lord,
In stark simplicity
Against the canopy
Of sapphire and pearl
You chose to unroll
This winter morning
And yet again
I am wowed
By the majesty
Of what seems ordinary
At best
To our self-absorbed eyes.
Be patient, I pray:
Teach me again, dear Lord,
To join the chorus
As all creation sings Your praise
And Your glory.

HOME

"Up a steep and very narrow stairway, to the voice like a metronome, up a steep and very narrow stairway, it wasn't paradise, it wasn't paradise, it wasn't paradise, but it was home."
—lyric by Edward Kleban, from At The Ballet, **A Chorus Line**.

This bit of song has been rolling
Drumming
Echoing
In my mind for two days now
Like feet running up those steep stairs
Like the counter's metered tick tick beat
The instructor's claps and calls to keep
The rhythm moving
Till I realized today
It was Your voice
Tapping
Through my waking and sleeping
Your voice, Master of the dance,
Subtly shifting my pace to Yours.

Home is many things:
Shelter to the unwanted.
Respect to the oppressed.
Embrace to the outcast.
A smile to the forgotten.
Hope to the disconsolate.
Faith to the doubtful.
A map to the lost.
Your lap. Your arms. Your breast.
   Your voice:
The familiar intimacy
The gentle crescendo of urgency
The invitation to join You
In the exhilarating dance
That leads home.
Where home *is* Paradise.

MIRACLES

In our cynical "Post Modern" view,
Science explains most mysteries,
Reason is more precious than belief,
And miracles just don't happen anymore
(Surprise, surprise)
Now that we understand cause and effect.
We take credit for inventions and insights,
For discoveries of how nature works
And new ways to promote healing or repair.
I wonder if You cry or laugh, Lord,
As we use lasers to clarify, cauterize or cut,
Forgetting that You are Light;
As we complain about the weather,
Neglecting to thank You for daily sunrise
And every precious drop of rain;
As we manufacture chips and circuits,
But never stop to praise You
For the remarkable properties of silicon,
Ores and petroleum—what used to be
Only sand, dirt and organic waste.
We correct vision every day,
Yet we are still blind
To Your miracles in plain sight.

December 13

SUN-BLIND

It happened again!
The drivers this morning
PANIC-
Stopped,
Blinded
By the fireball
That hovered on the horizon,
As if its appearance were
Unexpected,
Unforeseen,
Startling,
Even terrifying.
And I wondered,
For the zillionth time,
If they are so unprepared
For the sun's daily routine—
If they are so undone
By this mere reflection
Of You in Your creation—
How will they react, Lord,
In the actual
Overwhelming,
Unimaginable,
Awesome presence
Of Your spectacular glory?

COMPASS

New Brunswick Theological Seminary retreat, Lebanon, NJ.

As I spot the folded compass
Lying passive on the table
I see William Blake's painting:
God Almighty measuring out Creation
With the span of a compass
And a sober look of concentration
On his grey-trimmed brow.
This dimestore compass is pretty;
It seems handy enough
Except that, once taken up,
A pen is too broad for its barrel
And a pencil so narrow
It slips while marking only a few degrees
While the arc itself slides out
Like a puppy, legs splayed out,
Unable to sit, undisciplined,
And unaware of any purpose
To which I might set him.
I am no engineer
And this compass is no tool.
But in the hands of the Master Draftsman
I am a tool,
So I ask You to hold me steady
To the purpose You have in mind
That I may trace the arc
As You direct me.

December 15

QUIET

New Brunswick Theological Seminary retreat, Lebanon, NJ.

In the silence we have agreed to hold
The house is a comedy of sounds
A tumult of clownish noises—
The incessantly squealing radiator
The spurt gurgle psst! of its steam
The floorboards creak
The flames crack
Pages rustle as some sit reading
Others self-consciously snack:
Snap, nibble and chew.
There is the gentle shift of mostly burnt logs
The whoosh of water in the toilet overhead
The rattle of cold panes
In their old wood frames
As the arctic blast shoulders the door…
Hush.
Breathe.
Wait.
Listen to the candles
The coffee
The fire
Savor the sounds of life.

THE ROCK

New Brunswick Theological Seminary retreat, Lebanon, NJ.

The firebox is filled with flames
The old stones are charred black
Or bleached with ash.
My friend sits,
Sidled up to the hearth
Indian style,
In jeans and flannel plaid,
Intently studying a rock
Shaped and colored
Exactly like a potato,
Eyes and all,
Dimples he queries
Like a blind man
With his thumbs.
He hefts the rock,
Palm to palm,
Then cupped in both,
As if to test its worth;
And I wonder
If the rock is warmed
More by the fire
Or by his hands.
He places it on the granite hearth
Like a sacred offering upon an altar
And it gleams
Golden
Against the pewter slabs.

THE SHOFAR

New Brunswick Theological Seminary retreat, Lebanon, NJ.

The shofar—
A twist of horn
Like a misshapen Meerschaum
A kinked pipe
Whose bowl blows out
Instead of drawing in—
The shofar
Sits idle
Silent
Holding itself open
Ready
For someone
To give it breath
And then it will trumpet!
To spread the news
To summon the sleepers
To gather the scattered
To voice loud praise
For You
Our One and only
You
Who provided the ram.

MOGEN DAVID

New Brunswick Theological Seminary retreat, Lebanon, NJ.

Two triangles
Twice Trinity
Symmetry
Starburst, snowflake, emblem
Heraldry: pride of tribe and roots
Identity
Mark of joy
Turned to mark of sorrow
And shame
Torture
And death
Returned again—perfect
    symmetry?—
To symbol of pride
Sign of Hatikvah, the hope.
Tribe of David,
People of promise,
God's gift to the nations,
God's challenge to the world.
This star I hold is ceramic; it can
    be broken.
This star I hold is blue and white,
The traditional colors of Israel,
A broken people
A broken land
Yet the eternal, unshakable
    foundation
Of the Kingdom of God.
Star of David,
The banner of God's Anointed.
Like the cross,
It is a symbol of death
Transformed
Into the mark of Life.

CELEBRATION

We get so involved in holiday excitement,
Lord God, we let our focus slip away from You.
We are so busy celebrating with friends and family,
We forget to celebrate with You.
We forget the celebration *is* You!
We fall into the compelling routines of everyday.
We forget that You are the Life-Giver.
You are the Family-Maker.
You are the Provider of all we need.
You are the only Source of true joy.
Forgive us, I pray,
For neglecting You in the day-to-day,
For failing to acknowledge
You are the Author of all our blessings.
For moaning and groaning to each other
And failing to bring our concerns to You.
Help us to worship.
Help us to praise.
Help us to consult and to thank You
With every breath
Every day.

'TIS THE SEASON

Dear God,
We confess
I confess
We get caught up
In the business
And the busy-ness
Of this holiday season.
We forget
I forget
That "holiday" means holy day,
A time consecrated,
Dedicated in a special way,
To You.
We fret, we fume,
We get frazzled.
I sweat, I stew,
I get nasty in the crowds.
We feel short-tempered,
Short of funds,
And short on energy;
But in our hearts
We admit
I admit
We are, I am, really short on You.
Forgive us, Lord.
And teach us to give up anything
Everything
That keeps us from You.

RUMORS OF WAR

(Matthew 24:6)

We grow up with glory stories,
Gory details of brave warriors,
Self-sacrificing Everymen
Who gain mythological proportion
As they defeat the enemy
And save the day.
Drums, trumpets and banners
Quicken our pulse;
We hang our white hats
To ready our heads for harder gear.
We flex our muscle
We armor ourselves
We lock our knees
To stand against the foe
Forgetting that first
And always
We should bend them
In supplication to You,
For no one else
In heaven or earth
Can vanquish the evil
We wear in the name of good.

ORANGE ALERT: NEW YORK SUNDAY MORNING

From the calm though chatty
Suburban serenity
Of early morning worship
Passing quickly
(My pursuit rewarded)
Through the press of first crowds
At the just-opened Staples store,
Gliding down the empty highway
Through the police-protected tolls—
A ready-for-Action movie set—
The hollow tube under the Hudson
Open to flow with unaccustomed
Almost uneasy ease
Into the ever vibrant
Energetic
Always bustling City
Thrumming with traffic, taxis and tourists.
Jackhammers rip and crumble
At every corner
Cranes, backhoes, Bobcats rumble
And jive their unique jazz riffs...
All despite heightened alert
The supposed threat
And solemn warnings
That terror lurks.

Early to arrive,
I linger over coffee
At Mickey D's
Watching the faces
For signs of fear,
Finding only everyday grins
Or the occasional grimace;
Couples with no need to speak
Share their silence like food;
Laughing children, tired moms;
Singles find solace in their weighty *Times*
And an mid-morning mighty Mac.
Cell phones punctuate
The run-on sentences of routine noise.
I don't know what bothers me most, Lord,
That most people *live lives of quiet desperation*
Or that most people are oblivious
Complacent
Ignorantly unaware of
The presence
The prevalence
The pressure
The predatory pursuit
By evil.

RAINY DAY PRAYER

It's raining outside,
A dismal winter day;
There's static inside,
My radio won't play
The soothing classical hum
That usually smoothes my way.
But let storms and wind pelt
Roof, windows and walls,
Let accumulated snow melt
And ice warm into waterfalls,
Nothing can darken, steal
Or diminish my radiant joy!
For all life's pains, though real,
Are transitory. No evil ploy
Can undermine my faith in You,
My Lord, my Rock, my might;
Loud and clear Your voice comes through,
My courage, my comfort, my Light.

THIEF

It's not the ream of paper
He took without asking
From the credenza beside
   her desk,
Nor the promise to replenish
(When asked what he was doing)
And which remains a note unpaid.
It's about integrity;
It's a matter of respect.
He transgressed by ingress
With no thought to seek consent;
He breached the last wall of
   decency
By ignoring the presence
Of the occupant, the tenant
Of the space he violated,
The co-worker whose claim
To intrinsic value
Of territory
Of property
Of existence
He quashed
In a moment of petty larceny
And amplifies daily
By refusing,
Though reminded,
To keep his word
And replace
One lousy ream of paper.

When You heard the anger
I was rehearsing, Lord,
You stood before me,
Both wall and window,
And firmly said,
"Forgive him his debts."

YOUR GIFTS

How generous You are, Lord God!

You give us life and breath,
You make us each unique;
You give us life past death;
You call our hearts to seek
Faith, knowledge and truth.
You tell us in Your Word
We don't spring from primordial ooze
But were sculpted by You from earth.
You give us safety, water, food,
Clothing, sunlight and shade:
What we need for our own good,
And enough to share. You made
Us in Your likeness, so we are
Makers and givers, too. We paid
Nothing for these gifts. Like the star
Of Bethlehem, and the angels' praise,
Like the babe in the manger, Your Son,
Yourself. We have every reason to raise
Our voices in joyful thanks. He is the One
Whose birth we celebrate today
Whose return we anxiously await.

ALL THINGS NEW

A reflection on Luke 5:33-39

The Torah eaters are here again;
They claim to fast and beat their breast
Proudly in humble penitence
While they chew on the sacred scrolls
And on our misdemeanors.
They scratch their venerable beards
And belch in our faces,
Pleased to bless us with the stench
Of their self-important breath.
Like we're supposed to cave,
And beg to join their clan? *Not!*
Oh, sorry, Yesh; I know you're right.
I got carried away. I mean, look—
Oh! Yes, please tell me what to say
Next time they come on the prowl.

Let me try again: Sorry, guys, but it looks
Like you've confused tares and wheat here.

This is a celebration, and you're welcome to join;
Put away your sack and ash, don't even bother
To wash (and please don't tell us the rules!),
Just step into these party robes, grab a glass,
And join the dance! You've dined too long
On empty stalks, their shreds are stuck in your teeth.
Open your eyes! Fresh, succulent grainheads
Are ripe for the feast! Hear the music? Join
The dance! But watch you don't trip! Put aside
That old routine, watch and try a new pattern:
The choreography is, well, heaven! But it's
A total change—don't force your old steps,
Or you'll fall on your faces for sure! Trust
Me, fellas, if you're ready to make a change,
if you party with us, if you take a whirl
To the new tune, if you break bread with us
And toast the groom, I promise you this:
You'll catch the passion, you'll get the Word,
You'll be plugged in, you'll be new men!

THE PROCESS

Post-post-modern business
Switched the labels:
"Personnel" became "Human Resources"
So we should have seen it coming,
This depersonalization that turns
Bodies and souls into assets,
Capital, material goods, supplies.
In the Corporate thesaurus,
HR is a synonym of CYA,
A mathematical function of P&L.
The process used to be humane,
Gracious, respectful, cordial;
Now they process people like meat,
Grinding them up
And stuffing them—
Often into a place where they
Don't even fit, or
Leaving them on the side
To freeze. Or rust. Or rot.
Contingent on le whim du jour.
How hateful we are, dear Lord,
To allow our fellows to fall
Tragically far from the mark
With precious little protest.
We so fear our own loss of status,
We fail to see our apathetic limbs
Silently snatched into the blades.

INVISIBLE

At coffee hour I stood alone
In the midst of worshippers
Happily greeting each other
Pushing through the press
Of bodies and slamming me with
    elbows, purses, hips
Just as the coffee hit my lips
It seemed and I kept moving as
    though I were in the way
But even tucked off to the side,
    several folks found me—
Not as a newcomer to greet but
Rather an obstacle to overcome
If indeed they saw me at all.

At lunch I sat in a booth,
The left side of a back-to-back
Bench, the pleasure of my meal
Disturbed by the elbow, the arm,
The drumming fingers tossed
Thoughtlessly beside my head,
My face, my ear, by the man
    behind,
Who ignored my looks of
    discomfort,
My silent pleas to remove
    his limb,
To repair the breech. How ironic!
I thought, as I saw him stroll out
To a van proudly proclaiming
In bold black letters: WE CARE!

Without Your Spirit, Lord, how
Can we learn to see the invisible,
To hear the unspoken,
    uneasy pain
Of our neighbors, whom
    we paint
With transparent gloss and toss
Into the bin of oblivion?

FRUIT

My breakfast apple is perfect
Without blemish or bruise
It glistens and beckons a bite
But I choose the knife
To divide it neatly—
And behold the horror!
It's rotten to the core.
One quarter or less
Is fit for food. As I drop
The filth and wash the blade,
I hear You say, "So like you,
My child."

Forgive us, Lord.
We spend so much wealth,
    effort, time
Improving appearances,
Making perfect façades
To deflect from inner decay.
We perfect our teeth
With braces and bleach,
To better attract those we
    will chew.
We take lessons to sharpen our
    speech,
To ease doubts as we spread lies.
We pay trainers, dieticians,
    surgeons
To make us over into plastic
    ideals,
Preferring moments of shallow
    admiration
To the labor of forging
    friendship.
Forgive me, Lord, when I want
    to avoid
The piercing gaze of my fellows
Among the flawed yet
    flavorful fruit
Of Your fallen but redeemable
    world.

DEBRIS

With the gifts You gave us,
We've recreated the world.
Since what we did brought death
Anyway, we seem to think
Your work is wasted—
Just raw material for us
To sculpt into useful shapes,
To harvest and chop into fuel,
To redesign and decorate
With the detritus
Of our passing conquests.
Litter, graffiti, slums, slag,
Road kill, retreads, spent gum,
Books (who needs 'em?),
Last week's technology;
Rules? Regulations? Laws?
Ha! All fodder for the mill.
Nothing lasts, everything dies,
What's the point of old stones
Fashioned into smarter shape,
Museum looters seem to ask;
Goddess or spearhead, it'll
Fetch a buck or split a head;
Either way is just fine for us.
Let someone else clean up
The mess. You gotta break
Before you build, right?

SPRING FORWARD

Spring forward,
Fall back:
Our nursery rhyme
Measure to prime
A busy mind
To reset the time.
But it's also—
And how well You know,
Dear, patient God—
How we run our lives.
Jumping ahead
Before we consult with You,
Then falling back,
The inevitable consequence
Of our impetuous acts.
We seem to be more comfortable
In a fallen state,
But You know better,
And You keep picking us up
To begin again.

E.J. Emerson is a pastor living in New Jersey. She came to ministry at mid-life, after an interesting assortment of mostly writing, editing, marketing, and French translation work in the automotive, film, and biotech industries, with part-time positions teaching college freshman English.

By God's grace and healing hand, EJ is also a cancer survivor. In 2008, she came within a day of dying from a very rare lymphoma that had progressed to Stage IV without apparent symptoms.

She was healed literally overnight before the first dose of chemotherapy could possibly have had any effect. For this and many other blessings, EJ gives rousing thanks to God every day.

Edwards Brothers Inc.
Ann Arbor MI. USA
January 2, 2018